C A P S T O N E

D0558292

 INSTANT KNOWLEDGE

Stay Smart!

Smart things to know about... is a complete library of the world's smartest business ideas. **Smart** books put you on the inside track to the knowledge and skills that make the most successful people tick.

Each book brings you right up to speed on a crucial business issue. The subjects that business people tell us they most want to master are:

*Smart Things to Know about **Brands & Branding**,* JOHN MARIOTTI

*Smart Things to Know about **Business Finance**,* KEN LANGDON

*Smart Things to Know about **Change**,* DAVID FIRTH

*Smart Things to Know about **Customers**,* ROS JAY

*Smart Things to Know about **Decision Making**,* KEN LANGDON

*Smart Things to Know about **E-Commerce**,* MIKE CUNNINGHAM

*Smart Things to Know about **Innovation & Creativity**,* DENNIS SHERWOOD

*Smart Things to Know about **Knowledge Management**,* TOM M. KOULOPOULOS & CARL FRAPPAOLO

*Smart Things to Know about **Managing Projects**,* DONNA DEEPROSE

*Smart Things to Know about **Marketing**,* JOHN MARIOTTI

*Smart Things to Know about **Partnerships**,* JOHN MARIOTTI

*Smart Things to Know about **People Management**,* DAVID FIRTH

*Smart Things to Know about **Strategy**,* RICHARD KOCH

*Smart Things to Know about **Teams**,* ANNEMARIE CARACCIOLO

*Smart Things to Know about **Your Career**,* JOHN MIDDLETON

You can stay Smart by e-mailing us at info@wiley-capstone.co.uk
Let us keep you up to date with new Smart books, Smart updates, a Smart newsletter and Smart seminars and conferences. Get in touch to discuss your needs.

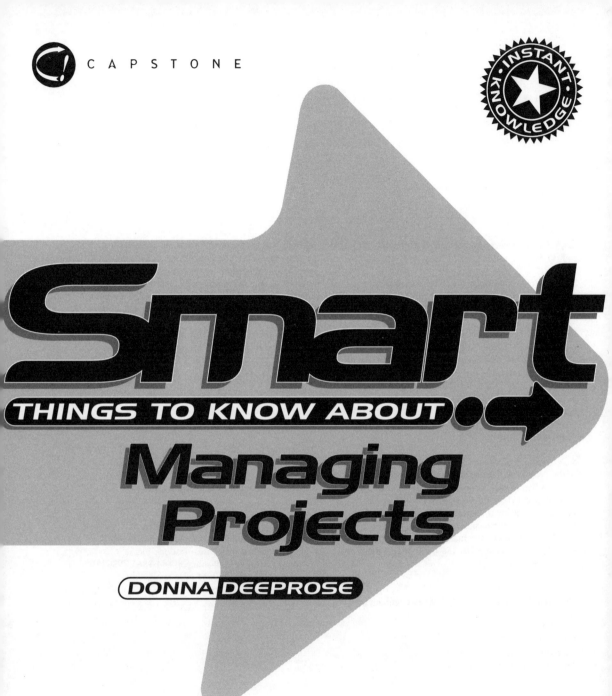

CAPSTONE

INSTANT · KNOWLEDGE

Smart

THINGS TO KNOW ABOUT

Managing Projects

DONNA DEEPROSE

Selections in this book are reprinted with permission of the Project Management Institute Headquarters, Four Campus Boulevard, Newtwon Square, PA 19073-2399 USA. Phone: (610) 356-4600, Fax: (610) 356-4647, Project Management Institute (PMI) is the world's leading project management association with over 70,000 members worldwide. For further information contact PMI Headquarters at (610) 356-4600 or visit the Web site at www.pmi.org.

First published 2001 by
Capstone Publishing Limited (A Wiley Company)
8 Newtec Place
Magdalen Road
Oxford OX4 1RE
United Kingdom
http://www.capstoneideas.com

CIP catalogue records for this book are available from the British Library and the US Library of Congress.

ISBN 1-84112-147-9

Typeset in 11/15pt Sabon by
Sparks Computer Solutions Ltd, Oxford, UK
http://www.sparks.co.uk

Printed and bound by
T.J. International Ltd, Padstow, Cornwall, UK

This book is printed on acid-free paper

Contents

Acknowledgements

I built this book upon the wisdom and experiences of people who are managing very exciting projects in corporations today, as well as some of the leading researchers and teachers in the field. For the time they spent talking to me, generously sharing the lessons they'd learned through hard work, I want to thank Greg Winsper and Andrew Gerson of AXA Client Solutions, Michael Walker of Estée Lauder, Julie Viscotti of Gartner, Mike Holveck of GlaxoSmithKline, Rick Zehner of Northwestern Mutual, Marie Scotto of The Scotto Group, Irwin Jacobs of Science Applications International Corporation, and noted authors and teachers, Dr Harold Kerzner of Baldwin-Wallace College, and Dr Hans Thamhain of Bentley College.

Some material in this book came from interviews I did earlier for other projects. Thanks again to Sherri Lindenberg and my long-time friend Eleanor Hamill of AXA, Karen Cone and Megan Taylor of Gartner, Mark Samuels and Murray Louis of SEI Investments, Jeff Ward of Celestica, and my pal and mentor Bill Becker, who shares his ideas generously and joyfully.

Writing a book is a project, and when I'm doing one, I need a project manager. Luckily, I have one to call on, my friend and colleague Rosalind Gold. I show up on her doorstep with a plea to organize me. She helps me draw up a plan of attack, creates a schedule for me, and prods, pushes, scolds, or cheers as required. Somehow she knows exactly when to say, "Stop thinking so hard and write. Call me in two hours and tell me you've finished that chapter." Or "Don't write anymore today. I won't allow it. Go outside." Since she runs workshops on both project management and business writing, she's also an expert manuscript reader. Roz, I can't thank you enough.

As always, my love and appreciation to my husband Ralph, who interrupted his own writing when I decided I needed a last-minute reader before sending off the manuscript.

What is Smart?

The *Smart* series is a new way of learning. *Smart* books will improve your understanding and performance in some of the critical areas you face today like *customers, strategy, change, e-commerce, brands, influencing skills, knowledge management, finance, teamworking,* and *partnerships*.

Smart books summarize accumulated wisdom as well as providing original cutting-edge ideas and tools that will take you out of theory and into action.

The widely respected business guru Chris Argyris points out that even the most intelligent individuals can become ineffective in organizations. Why? Because we are so busy working that we fail to learn about ourselves. We stop reflecting on the changes around us. We get sucked into the patterns of behavior that have produced success for us in the past, not realizing that it may no longer be appropriate for us in the fast-approaching future.

There are three ways the *Smart* series helps prevent this happening to you:

- by increasing your self-awareness;

- by developing your understanding, attitude and behavior; and

- by giving you the tools to challenge the status quo that exists in your organization.

Smart people need smart organizations. You could spend a third of your career hopping around in search of the Holy Grail, or you could begin to create your own smart organization around you today.

Finally a reminder that books don't change the world, people do. And although the *Smart* series offers you the brightest wisdom from the best practitioners and thinkers, these books throw the responsibility on you to *apply* what you're learning in your work.

Because the truly smart person knows that reading a book is the start of the process and not the end …

As Eric Hoffer says, "In times of change, learners inherit the world, while the learned remain beautifully equipped to deal with a world that no longer exists."

David Firth
Smartmaster

Preface

There was a time when professional progress was typically linear. You went to work, performed a certain function, got better and better at it, and gradually expanded your range of expertise. When you got really good at your job, you were promoted to manage other people doing the same or similar work.

The work itself evolved to keep up with new technology and shifts in customer demands. But, pretty much, your course was predictable. What you expected to do tomorrow and next year was what you'd been doing yesterday and last year, albeit with refinements and gradually increasing complexity.

It's not like that anymore! (But you already know that or you wouldn't be looking at this book.)

Now business is all about change – catching up with it, riding it, staying ahead of it. And work is all about projects to make change happen. Moving from project to project means that what you are doing today may be totally different from what you did last year and from what you will be doing next month or next year. It's less like the old scientific management school, which dominated most of the last century, focused on reducing change to a minimum for efficiency's sake, and more like the engineering/construction model, based on the principle that every body of work has a specific beginning, when the contract is signed, and a specific end, when the building or bridge or dam is complete.

The movement toward project management as a business model is nothing short of a revolution. And you, whether you volunteered or were conscripted, are a revolutionary.

Part I
The Project Management Revolution

Where did it come from, this revolution that is infiltrating even the most functionally organized companies? How different is it really from the traditional model? And what changes does it demand from us in order to join it? This part of the book answers those questions to build a foundation for the how-to chapters that follow.

Chapter 1, *It's Not Just for Engineers Anymore*, investigates why and how all kinds of businesses are adapting project management tools and techniques to their own use.

Chapter 2, *Projects vs. Operations*, uncovers the similarities and underscores the differences between project and operations management.

1

It's Not Just for Engineers Anymore

In years to come, many companies will look back on this time as one of transition between *BPM* and *APM*. That's Before Project Management and Advent of Project Management.

In the dark ages of *BPM*, when a good idea arose in an organization, management appointed a task force to study its feasibility and make recommendations. After that various functional departments battled over who would or wouldn't own the initiative: *would* if it was a high profile undertaking with a high chance of success; *wouldn't* if it looked like somebody's screwball scheme that would never succeed or if it involved lots of work and little budget. Most companies tell horror stories from that era. In a giant insurance company, people remember not long ago when the marketing department churned out product materials without any input from the sales force. Hence no sales people ever used them.

Hans Thamhain, professor of management at Bentley College in Waltham/ Boston, Massachusetts, puts project management into an historical perspective. "It's not really a thing invented in the last ten years," he reminds us. "When they built the pyramids or the first irrigation systems – those were big projects. They didn't have to go to engineering school and read books about it.

"But we can't do it by trial and error and luck anymore. We have to have threshold competency whether for large or small projects. Some small projects, such as Web site development, are critical. The business success of the company can depend upon them."

Enter cross-functional teams. By pulling together representatives of every part of the organization with a stake in the outcome, such teams transcend turf issues. But project success requires more than cooperation. It demands skills in project definition, planning, and controlling more systematic and precise than most functional managers have ever needed to apply to their ongoing operations. Absent those skills, even the best-intentioned cross-functional team can flounder in disarray.

A team in a software company owned by a brokerage firm struggled fruitlessly for a year and a half in an effort to create software for trading. Finally, they brought in an external project management consultant to help them get on track. She found them overwhelmed by the magnitude of their charge, having never prioritized their requirements, nor broken the project into approachable chunks with manageable outcomes.

An internal project management consultant in a Fortune 500 company recalls a desperate group of people charged with designing a new compensation plan for the company sales force. But there was no document defining the project scope. So months into the effort with the deadline looming, the team members were all scattered in different directions, doing what they each thought was the right thing. Five different external consultants had been hired to do the same work. But none of them had defined deliverables. In fact, the team was hopelessly lost in a labyrinth of unintegrated activities.

Project management to the rescue

Michael Holveck, who heads up the project management function within the Office of Change Management at GlaxoSmithKline in Research Triangle Park, North Carolina, lives right on the *BPM/APM* cusp. Holveck talks about initiatives, not projects, because at GlaxoSmithKline the word "project" still smacks of "geeky engineers with pocket protectors."

But geeky or not, engineers had project management skills that others in the company began to eye covetously. Holveck was in the Engineering Department at GlaxoWellcome (which merged with SmithKline Beecham in 2000 to form GlaxoSmithKline) when the company's sales and marketing arm sent out a plea for help. Could someone from Engineering help manage a project to redesign the sales and marketing processes? It was a colossal initiative involving a core team and seven sub-teams. Holveck volunteered, joining the core team.

On his first day, Holveck recalls, he pulled out his bag of engineering tricks: scope statements, Gantt Charts, technology for controlling processes, reporting methodologies. As he describes it, "the typical way engineering/ construction would control capital projects."

The executive in charge of the process redesign looked at him and said, "You know I don't think we're ready for this. What I'd like you to do is help with the organization and the scope definition in a way that doesn't scare the bejeesus out of my colleagues." Holveck scaled back his approach.

But three months later the core team sat in a room listening to the seven sub-team leaders struggle with inter-team problems. They talked about how each team was dependent upon the others. How one team couldn't get started on something until another team had completed something else. How they needed to bring in outside consultants, but couldn't until they'd done at least two other things beforehand.

Finally someone turned to the leader of the whole initiative and said, "We really need an integrated plan for this."

The leader smiled and said, "I think Mike can help with this."

Holveck smiled back and replied, "Yes, I think I can."

SMART VOICES

Sherri Lindenberg, vice-president of AXA Client Solutions in New York and an experienced project manager, calls working in project teams "operating outside the red tape."

Recalling that project, which lasted 18 months, Holveck adds, "I won't say we used all the project management tools, but most of the processes got implemented. When it was over, the project manager stood up in front of senior management and said if he had to do it over again, he'd implement project management tools right at the beginning."

These days, operating from the Office of Change Management in the recently merged pharmaceutical giant, Holveck gets to implement project management tools from the beginning of most of the organization's strategic change initiatives. Holveck's group worked on over 100 initiatives in a single year.

The dawn of a new era

GlaxoSmithKline isn't the only company where project management is not just for engineers anymore. The Estée Lauder Companies Inc. is another

example of an organization where project management methodology is spreading throughout the company. Michael Walker, director of Capital Budgeting and Project Management in the Corporate Engineering Department in Melville, New York, says that a growing proportion of the cosmetic company's manufacturing capital budget is being managed through projects. And a number of other groups are follow manufacturing's example.

The project management bible, *A Guide to the Project Management Body of Knowledge (PMBOK® Guide,* affectionately pronounced "pimbok") acknowledges a movement toward managing by projects in functional organizations. These organizations, it finds, "treat many aspects of ongoing operations as projects in order to apply project management to them."[1]

Management guru Tom Peters, author of *The Project 50 (Reinventing Work): Fifty Ways to Transform Every "Task" into a Project That Matters!*, goes a step further and declares that all white-collar work is – or should be – project work. Traditional ways of working are too slow, he insists, and too hard to place a value on. Projects, he asserts, make it possible for white-collar workers to demonstrate convincingly that they add value.

What exactly is a project?

Well then, if we're on the threshold of the age of project management, and especially if Tom Peters is right that all white-collar work is being reinvented into project work, we'd better define exactly what projects are before we move forward with guidelines for managing them.

A project is the work that needs to be done to produce a unique, predefined outcome within a predetermined period of time and budget.

Its *one-of-a-kind* nature distinguishes it from the *ongoing* work that Peters decries for being slow and hard to value, but that most of us still toil at much of the time.

Designing a new Web site is a project that's over once it is up and online with the initial bugs cleaned out. Maintaining that Website with new material every week is not a project; it's ongoing work. If you redesign it a year later, that's a new project.

The scrapbook on comets you did for science class in grade school – creating that was a project. Reading ten pages per week of your high school science textbook and answering questions on it – that was ongoing work.

Smart quotes

The *PMBOK® Guide* defines project as "*a temporary endeavor under-taken to create a unique product or service.*" *Temporary* means that every project has a definite beginning and a definite end. *Unique* means that the product or service is different in some distinguishing way from all similar products or services."

The *PMBOK® Guide* further clarifies that, while the project is temporary, the result usually isn't. "For example, a project to erect a national monument will create a result expected to last centuries."[3]

Getting everyone in your office to spend an afternoon pitching in to clear out a bank of overflowing file cabinets – even that is a project. Keeping the cabinets from filling up again is ongoing work.

Been there, done that ... haven't I?

OK, it's pretty obvious we've all handled projects, from creating scrapbooks to arranging family reunions. If you are married, you know what a project the wedding was! (The wedding was the project; staying married is ongoing work.) So why do we have to borrow a bag of tricks from engineers to handle projects when we've been doing it all our lives? Because:

- *Handle* them is just what we did. Managing them is a degree of magnitude richer, more efficient, and more effective.

- With each work project you complete successfully, you'll probably be expected to take on another of increasing complexity until your projects grow well beyond what you can manage by the seat of your pants. Without good project management skills you'll find yourself and your project team strangled by conflicting priorities, stuck on a dead-end route, running off in divergent directions, or caught in an endless loop that gets you no nearer your goal.

Quite often, people misunderstand the concept … In such a case, the following might be considered an appropriate definition:

Project management is the art of creating the illusion that any outcome is the result of a series of predetermined, deliberate acts when, in fact, it was dumb luck.

Although this might be the way that some companies are running their projects, this is not project management.

Harold Kerzner, PhD, *Project Management: A Systems Approach to Planning, Scheduling, and Controlling,* 7th edition[4]

- Project management is not really a bag of tricks. It's the application of validated processes and tested tools that require discipline but reward you with a clear route to your goal and the ability to make course corrections with the least amount of pain when uncharted volcanoes suddenly erupt and spew lava over your path. And while you must follow the processes, you can pick and choose the tools that work best for you.

- While you may be able to muscle your way through one project, what will you do when you find yourself juggling two or three, while being expected to stay current with your ongoing work?

Working off the side of your desk

Take another look at the final bullet above. Does that remind you of anyone you know – yourself, perhaps? If you are not working that way now, you probably will be soon. In *BPM* days, managers devoted themselves to attaining their work unit priorities and developing the people who worked for them. But even then they were occasionally charged with heading up a special project that crossed departmental lines. As AXA Client Solutions vice-president Sherri Lindenberg once said, they worked that project "off the side of their desk."

But that has changed. Now that companies have found cross-functional project teams to be the fastest, most efficient, and most effective way to accomplish high-impact goals, both managers and employees are spending more time on special projects. What's happening now, Lindenberg observed, is that it's often the old job that gets done off the side of the desk rather than the new projects.

It's a way of life for managers and employees in companies everywhere. At Estée Lauder, Mike Walker, PMP, confirms, it's not unusual for a part-time project manager to have between six and ten active projects. On top of that she may be a team member on somebody else's project because of her functional expertise. A maintenance supervisor, for example, may lead a project for acquiring new equipment, contribute his maintenance knowledge to three other teams as a team member, and all the while continue to be responsible for the ongoing maintenance of existing equipment.

Smart quotes

[Project] teams can take your eye off your main responsibility or other projects on which you may be working ... You may need to prioritize which project (if you are working on more than one) will be smartest for the business and your personal benefit.

Annemarie Caracciolo, *Smart Things To Know About Teams*[5]

GlaxoSmithKline's Mike Holveck describes the balancing act and its risks for both individuals and organizations: "The best people get assigned to be implementation leaders [GlaxoSmithKline's terminology for project managers] over and over again until they are maxed out. And, oh, by the way, they still have to do their regular jobs."

Good project management is as much about managing time and commitments as it is about defining and scheduling tasks.

Make no mistake. *APM* is here now. So borrow all you can from the engineers' bag of tricks to equip yourself because, as Tom Peters would say, You = Your Projects. From now on you'll have to manage: first, "Project You"; second, work initiatives with precise goals and limited lifespans; and third, an ongoing function related to your technical expertise.

Without good project-management skills, that would be an impossible juggling task.

The smartest things in this chapter

- A project is the work that needs to be done to produce a unique, predefined outcome within a predetermined period of time and budget.

- Project management is using validated processes and tested tools to map a route to a goal and make course corrections as you travel it.

- In many organizations it is not unusual for one person to lead a project, be a team member on a few more, and manage ongoing work all at the same time.

Notes

1 *A Guide to the Project Management Body of Knowledge*, 1996 ed. Newtown Square, PA: copyright © 1996 Project Management Institute.

2 Quoted from the May 1999 issue of *Fast Company* magazine. All rights reserved.

3 *A Guide to the Project Management Body of Knowledge*, 1996 ed. Newtown Square, PA: copyright © 1996 Project Management Institute.

4 Kerzner, H. *Project Management: A Systems Approach to Planning, Scheduling, and Controlling*, 7th ed. New York: copyright © 2000 Harold Kerzner. Reprinted by permission of John Wiley & Sons, Inc.

5 Caracciolo, A.M. *Smart Things to Know About Teams*, Oxford: Capstone, 2000.

2

Projects vs. Operations

When they compare managing projects with managing operations, most books start with the differences between the two. It's true the differences are eye-opening. But instead of trying to frighten you into unlearning a whole set of behaviors that worked for you in the past, this chapter is going to start with the *similarities* between projects and operations.

If you've been managing a work unit, or even observed the behaviors of effective work unit managers, you have certain skills and knowledge you can transfer to a project. So let's start by acknowledging your strengths. (We'll get around to the differences and all you're going to have to learn in due time after you are confident that you have some basics to build on.)

Transferable skills

Unlike many companies, Northwestern Mutual, a financial services company specializing in life insurance in Milwaukee, Wisconsin, has always had a project mentality. Ask people there how long they've had project teams and they are likely to reply, "Well, the company is about 140 years old ... " Ask Rick Zehner, vice-president of Marketing, about similarities and differences between projects and operations, and he begins by saying, "Ultimately, whether it's a project or an operating unit, you are managing people and a budget."

Smart things to say about managing projects

Some people say you manage a work unit, but you lead a project team. But if you are just "managing" your work unit according to the criteria they suggest, you're doing that job by some very outmoded standards. If you are a good work unit manager you are already empowering your employees to innovate and solve problems. If you aren't doing those things, you need to develop those skills not just for leading your project but for managing your work unit as well.

Whether you are leading an operating unit or a project team, a big component of your job is:

- *Managing people.* Rule number one is to set clear accountabilities. If you've got a good performance-management system in your organization, you already know that people's performance improves when they know from the beginning of the performance cycle what their goals are and exactly what is expected of them. That works with project team members, too. In fact, it is even more crucial when projects are large, with responsibilities spread among various sub-teams, emphasizes Zehner, who led Northwestern Mutual's corporate-wide Brand Equity Project.

- *Managing a budget.* Your job is to figure out what it's going to cost to perform the necessary work and to accomplish your objectives – whether project goals or annual work unit goals – without spending more than you estimated.

- *Communicating with the team, with upper management, with outside stakeholders.* This shouldn't surprise those operations managers who have learned the value to their work unit's success (and their own career advancement) of keeping upper management, their peers, and their workers well informed of all issues that affect work unit performance, and of listening to information and insights from others.

- *Staying flexible.* If you are managing an operations unit or even working in one, you've learned to swing with the punches and land on your feet throughout upheavals in company priorities, flip-flops in market conditions, unanticipated personnel movements, and any number of unforeseen changes. You are going to need all those coping skills, because projects are rife with the unexpected.

Just when you think it's going to be easy

By now you should be feeling pretty confident that you've got a lot going for you. You've had experience in managing people, managing a budget, communicating relentlessly, and staying flexible. But here's the rub: all those things take on new twists when you are managing a project, which by definition is temporary and unique instead of ongoing and repetitive.

This is not to suggest that your ongoing work never changes. Of course it does. Now and then you drop a task by handing it off to someone else or because it no longer serves the organization's purposes. For the most part, though, change means your job grows. You get new assignments all the time, assignments that you are expected to add permanently to your work.

Smart quotes

The vertical flow of work is still the responsibility of the line managers. The horizontal flow of work is the responsibility of the project managers, and their primary effort is to communicate and coordinate activities horizontally between the line organizations.

Harold Kerzner, *Project Management: A Systems Approach to Planning, Scheduling, and Controlling*, 7th edition[1]

The big difference

But project work is all start-up work. (If it begins to look permanent, the project is in big trouble.) The purpose of the project is to create something, usually a product or service. The project ends when the product or service is launched, tested, and declared operational. From beginning to end, the life of a project looks like this:

Four phases of a project

	Key deliverables		
Conceptualization*	Planning*	Delivery*	Closure*
Project charter. Agreement on the purpose, intended outputs, and scope of the project. Constraints and assumptions you are operating under. Core project team. Commitment of all the stakeholders.	Project plan including project deliverables, tasks to be done, schedule, assignments, contingency plan, communication plan, and budget.	Status reports. Project review meetings. Change requests. Updates to project plan, schedule, and budget. Milestones achieved.	All deliverables to fulfill project goals. Final financial accounting. Full documentation of project. Final reports to customers and management. Celebration.

* These names come from GlaxoSmithKline. In other books you may find the Conceptualization phase called Initiating and the Delivery stage broken into two, often called Executing and Controlling. We like the term Conceptualization because it emphasizes that this is the thinking part, when you really have to conceive, analyze, synthesize, and figure out just what this project needs to accomplish and how. We like Delivery because it has a proactive, positive tone, and because from a project manager's point of view, it's pretty hard to separate executing from controlling.

The product or service created may then go on and on. But at that point, it's no longer a project, it's part of operations. If you continue to work on it, your mindset shifts back to operations management mode.

Now let's look at how the temporary nature of projects changes how you work.

Managing the project way

The most obvious difference is the increased emphasis on planning. In operations, you might write an annual business plan, but that is more about what you are going to do than how you are going to do it. That works because for the most part, you follow tried and true methods and do tasks you have done before.

But a project, because it is both new and time-bound, requires a plan of exquisite specificity and detail. When you get the plan right, a lot of project managers will tell you, the rest is easy. (Of course it's not easy, but what they really mean is, "The rest is *possible*.")

Beyond the planning difference, there are also significant changes in how, as a project manager, you will perform the functions that projects and operations share:

- *Managing people.* By an old definition, management is "getting work done through other people." Project managers usually have to get work done through people who don't report to them. Most project teams are made up of people from various parts of the organization lent to the project part-time. Their first commitment

Smart quotes

Projects are fundamentally different because the project ceases when its declared objectives have been attained, while non-project undertakings adopt a new set of objectives and *continue* to work.

The *PMBOK® Guide*[2]

SMART VOICES

The first difference between managing a work unit and managing a project is that you have no authority over individuals other than your good will.

Michael Walker,
Estée Lauder

is to their ongoing job. Their first loyalty is to their work unit manager. They'll devote themselves wholeheartedly to a project not out of duty, but only out of passion. It's the project manager's job to instill that passion for the project not only in the team members but also, to a degree, in the members' work unit managers, who must sign off on the team members' participation in the first place and whose willingness to lend their employees must be continually renewed.

On generating passion and winning commitment:

The key is making sure upfront that there is ownership in the project. Here's what I've found to be successful. In the early stages I put together a strategy session and invite people I think will become members of the team. I pick influential managers who, I think, will be passionate about this opportunity. The day is used to brainstorm. We have an agenda; it's not loosey goosey. By the time I sum up the meeting and ask what they think, they see that they've already put a mark on it. By the end of the day, most people in the room are asking, "Where can I sign up?" They get excited and get their people excited.

Greg Winsper, AXA Client Solutions

- *Managing a budget.* Expect to do a lot more homework before you write a project budget than you usually do for your operations budget. In operations, you can look at your budget from last year and tweak it to meet this year's new restrictions or opportunities. For a project, you start from scratch. And as an experienced project manager, Greg Winsper, head of AXA Client Solutions' Relationship Distribution Group in New York warns, "You don't want to get stuck under-budgeting because it's a lot more difficult to go back and ask for more."

Executing that budget takes some new skills too, especially when your project touches a lot of different areas of the company. Northwestern

Mutual's Rick Zehner recalls the complexities of managing the budget for the company's branding project: "Although it was my budget, it was spent by a lot of different areas in the company. We had to go through a prioritization process to determine what departments were going to get what parts of the budget. For example, we have marketing materials produced by different product lines – life, disability, long-term care, etc. We had to decide which of the materials were going to get funded first."

- *Communicating.* The magnitude of the communications required will seem exponentially greater when you manage a project, especially if it's a corporate-wide initiative with implications touching departments as far-ranging as legal, compliance, training, technology, human resources, and various product lines. And once you get started on a cross-functional project, you'll be amazed to discover just how many areas you need to interact with.

Rick Zehner describes some of the communications that Northwestern Mutual's branding project required: "We had one sub-team focused just on change management communication, but it still took a great deal of my own time, and it could have been 150 percent. We did a lot of communication with senior management, getting in front of them almost on a weekly basis. I was going to those meetings and getting feedback directly from them. There were meetings with members of the company's distribution system, and formal briefings with all employees. We also used a lot of other devices, such as our internal newsletter and internal news program. Within the different product areas, they have their own communications vehicles, perhaps monthly newsletters. In addition, there was a whole lot of communications to policy owners, consumers in general, and the media."

- *Staying flexible.* Since each project is unique, project teams are often treading new ground, following road maps based more on best guesses

Harold Kerzner, professor of systems management at Baldwin-Wallace College in Berea, OH, and executive director, International Institute of Learning, tells a story to emphasize how leading a project team differs from leading an operations work group:

"A giant telecommunications company asked me to draw up a project management curriculum for them. They looked over the list and told me to take out all the behavioral topics. They said they had a series of courses on how to become a first-line supervisor covering the same topics, and participants would all have gone through it.

"I went to the HR people and asked 'In your courses for first-line managers, do you discuss the principles of leadership?' They answered, 'Yes.'

'Do you cover leading subordinates or leading people who don't report to you?'

'Leading subordinates,' they answered.

'Do you cover motivation?' I asked. Again the answer was yes.

'Motivating subordinates or motivating people who don't report to you?'

'Motivating subordinates,' was the reply.

"Finally they realized that all their traditional courses were predicated on the superior/subordinate relationship. But there's a complicating factor for project managers. For one thing, usually the boss earns more money than the employees. That's not necessarily so for project managers. They may have people on the team who earn more than they do and rank higher in the organization. How do you provide motivation and conflict resolution to people three pay grades higher than you are?"

That's the kind of question that rivets Dr Kerzner these days, after more than 35 years practicing, studying, and teaching project management and authoring 18 books on the subject, including *Project Management: A Systems Approach to Planning, Scheduling, and Controlling.*

Hard lessons

To reach that understanding, he says, project-management practitioners had to learn some hard lessons. "Historically, when a project was in trouble, the problem was blamed on poor planning and scheduling – all the quantitative techniques. But finally we began to realize that the real problems were poor morale, poor interactivity, poor leadership, and poor support by line managers. The majority of projects we wrote off were because of behavioral failures.

"If the behaviors are in place, you can take the worst possible plan and make it successful. But you can develop the greatest plan and if the people aren't motivated, they'll take you and your plan and bury you with it."

The organizational side

As focused as he is on both the quantitative and leadership skills of project managers, Dr Kerzner is equally absorbed in the organizational side of project management. "Companies realized that project management resulted in accomplishing more work in less time with fewer people," he says. "So they began to think, 'Maybe we can use it for smaller projects.' That has led to three trends:

- Increased strategic planning for project management. Those companies with centralized project reporting systems, e.g. through an intranet, are using the information they acquire to assess how much business to take on and where to apply resources.
- Application of a single project-management methodology across the company. The search for the best methodology to use contributes to the third trend:
- Benchmarking, not just to copy what companies are doing now, but to project what project management will be like in the future."

Dr Kerzner asserts that "A lot of companies are realizing that project management is the survival of the firm. They want to sell their products and services to customers. They are saying, 'We provide solutions.' To sell a solution, they have to have project management skills to deliver."

than on past experience. On projects, in fact, swinging with the punches isn't enough; you'd probably get dizzy and fall. On a project, staying flexible doesn't mean going with the flow. It means being ready for the unexpected by planning completely and meticulously and keeping on top of emerging problems. It means analyzing the risks in advance and building contingencies into your project plan. Flexibility is a lot easier and more effective when you have an alternative plan ready to put into action.

And now for the good news

Project management may be different, but, many practitioners say, it also offers some advantages that you may not have as an operations manager. At least, if you set your project up carefully in advance, you should have:

- *Senior management commitment.* In companies like Estée Lauder, AXA, and Northwestern Mutual, the process of approval for cross-functional projects ensures senior management support. The key thing is having a sponsor, an individual at a high enough level to influence the commitment of all stakeholders, who is as passionate about the project as are the project manager and team members.

- *Some control over who is on your team.* When you take over the management of a work unit, you usually inherit its employees. With a project team, you start with a blank slate and can at least ask for the people you know will do the best job. Will you have to accept some substitutes? Sure, but there's a good chance you can gather a core group you know you can count on.

- *Control over meeting agendas.* If this sounds small, trust the experience of Northwestern Mutual's Rick Zehner. "Meetings," he says, "are a great method for maintaining discipline over the process. People have to come and talk about what they are doing. Because you don't have formal power, you need some other mechanisms working for you, and this is a good one." Of course, you could use this in operations also, but people do tend to avoid department meetings in favor of tasks. As a project manager, use meetings to your advantage.

Are you ready to join the revolution?

You might think of this book as a recruiting manual for project management revolutionaries. It's time to sign up if:

- Your organization has caught project fever and is turning its most exciting initiatives over to cross-functional project teams rather than dealing them out to individual operations units. Or if you want to start your own revolution by championing a cross-functional project team to achieve a goal that goes beyond your functional limits.

- You've got basic skills for managing people, resources, communications, and planning. Or you want to develop those skills.

- You want to learn how to expand those skills to tackle the special challenges of managing a project, which is temporary, unique, and highly goal-driven, rather than ongoing and repetitive.

Your training begins with the next chapter.

The smartest things in this chapter

- Project management requires planning at a level of detail and precision seldom applied in operations.

- Project managers must get work done through people who do not report to them.

- Project managers can be flexible if they have analyzed risks in advance and developed contingency plans.

- Project management success depends upon maintaining regular communications with a wide group of managers, employees, customers, and other stakeholders.

Notes

1   Kerzner, H. *Project Management: A Systems Approach to Planning, Scheduling, and Controlling*, 7th ed. New York: copyright © 2000 Harold Kerzner. Reprinted by permission of John Wiley & Sons, Inc.

2   *A Guide to the Project Management Body of Knowledge*, 1996 ed. Newtown Square, PA: copyright © 1996 Project Management Institute.

Part II
The Science of Managing Projects

Scientists have processes to follow and tools to use. So do project managers. This part of the book is about the processes, techniques, and tools that project managers use to transform a bright idea into a sound business success.

Chapter 3, *The Birth of a Project*, focuses on the Conceptualization Phase, looking at the processes and procedures you'll need to follow and the project charter you'll need to write. It provides various examples you can crib from to create the charter that is right for you.

Chapter 4, *A Carefully Crafted Plan*, takes you to the heart of the planning process and provides samples of the tools experienced project managers use to make their work easier.

Chapter 5, *Making Sense out of Dollars*, tackles the money issue, with guidelines for estimating costs and preparing a budget.

Chapter 6, *Making It Happen*, is about doing the work, tracking progress against goals, and making adjustments when necessary to stay on target.

3
The Birth of a Project

You probably pride yourself on being a can-do person who spots a problem and takes steps to solve it fast. So heed this: the first lesson of project management is to suppress your bias for action.

Every project has a gestation period, when you think it through carefully, define it precisely, and line up the support you'll need to bring the project to fruition. To shortchange this stage is to court disaster. (And the truth is that the first stage is followed by a planning period when you still have to restrain your urge to act now and think later.)

To put this chapter in context, let's take another look at the phases of project management introduced in Chapter 2.

SMART VOICES

Most people are prone to action. The first thing someone wants to do is do something – start moving bricks or writing programming code. That's the downfall of a lot of projects.

Mike Walker, Estée Lauder Companies

How do I get started?

Exactly what am I expected to achieve?

Who is responsible for what, and how am I supposed to coordinate the effort?

Michael C. Thomsett, *The Little Black Book of Project Management*[1]

	Key deliverables		
Conceptualization	Planning	Delivery	Closure
Project charter. Agreement on the purpose, intended outputs, and scope of the project. Constraints and assumptions you are operating under. Core project team. Commitment of all the stakeholders.	Project plan including project deliverables, tasks to be done, schedule, assignments, contingency plan, communication plan, and budget.	Status reports. Project review meetings. Change requests. Updates to project plan, schedule, and budget. Milestones achieved.	All deliverables to fulfill project goals. Final financial accounting. Full documentation of project. Final reports to customers and management. Celebration.

Smart quotes

If you don't understand the question, you cannot possibly be expected to find the solution. Nor can you plan or manage the project.

Joan Knutson and Ira Blitz, *Project Management: How to Plan and Manage Successful Projects*[2]

Project gestation occurs during the Conceptualization Phase. Restraining your bias for action at this phase definitely doesn't mean sitting and contemplating your navel, waiting for inspiration to strike. It does mean resisting the urge to leap to a solution. Instead, this is a time to concentrate on accurately defining the problem or opportunity, narrowing it to specific, measurable goals, and assessing and shaping the context in which you will pursue those goals. In the process, the project can change considerably from your first kernel of an idea.

HOW A *GOOD* IDEA GREW … AND GREW

Northwestern Mutual Life, headquartered in Milwaukee, Wisconsin, was a venerable company with a proud history that dated back to its founding in 1857. But by the late 1990s, it had moved into a range of financial activities that far outspanned the image suggested by its name and the perception most people had of the company. The company needed to create a new brand that integrated its entire portfolio of products and services and responded to the urging from members of the field force to update their image as one-product providers.

The Management Committee tapped Rick Zehner, who was in corporate planning at the time, to lead a fledgling branding project, to be known as the Brand Equity Project. The definition of the project given to him was restricted to positioning the company relative to consumers.

Zehner plunged into what he calls a "discovery process." A project, he explains, typically starts out with someone taking a leadership role, doing a rough cut of the project charter, and walking around to get feedback from key stakeholders. Talking to one stakeholder often leads to the identification of more, so the task wears out a lot of shoe leather. For the branding project, it also garnered a wealth of ideas for broadening the project scope. Still, the charter that Zehner and his boss – the project sponsor – wrote for the management committee stuck to the original purpose. But by the time they came out of the management committee meeting, after a full discussion of the needs they'd uncovered, the project had grown from one objective to so many that Zehner jokes he couldn't remember them. Ultimately they simplified it to three – to answer these questions:

- Who are we in the minds of our target market customers and what *do* we want to be?
- How do we best manage our portfolio brands?
- What is the best way to present what our field force does to our target market consumers in terms most relevant to them?

At the same time, the team grew from Zehner's requested four members to a core of nine, and the project expanded to permeate almost every part of the company.

To begin at the beginning

Where do most project ideas come from?

- *From you, perhaps.* Here's a scenario: You're working away at your job one day when, *voilà*, a light bulb appears over your head. Suddenly you have a vision of a brand new product that will revolutionize your industry. All you need is the cooperation of a designer, a few programmers, and, well, maybe R&D and the marketing department ... but it will work. You just know it, and nobody's ever thought of it before.

  OK, here's a more likely scenario. You and some colleagues are sitting in the lunchroom grumbling as usual about some glitch in the system that constantly slows you down. "We oughta put our heads together and solve this," someone says. Someone else pulls out a pen and starts to scribble numbers and diagrams on a napkin. You lean over and add a few arrows, getting into the act. "We could do it, you know," you assert, now getting enthusiastic, "if we could just grab a programmer or two, and maybe someone from production and maintenance."

  Those things happen, and out of them project teams are born. A Motorola plant outside Chicago decorated its walls with pictures of successful teams that each began with some worker's great idea for a product improvement. At SEI Investments in New Jersey, important new initiatives begin because a few people get to talking and discover they are all wrestling with the same problem. Conversations like that led to a company-sanctioned new career path for a group of service employees whose career options were restricted. They also led to the creation of a new research function in the organization.

- *From customers.* Other great project ideas come from casual comments of outside customers. A couple of SEI's banking clients expressed interest in taking their investment vehicles onto the Internet. That led to an SEI project to build a Web site that could be customized to each client.

- *From upper management.* In fact, most projects you'll take part in will come down to you from up above. (That doesn't mean they all originated there. Senior management may be responding to a need that's bubbled up from the troops.) Someone in upper management taps you to lead or participate in a project team to solve a problem or pursue an opportunity with implications that extend far beyond your own department.

A good place to start

So you've got a great idea. Now what are you going to do with it? If you can, get help. Gather a small group of people, preferably people with as much stake in the outcome as you have, to work with you right from the start.

You don't want a cast of thousands here (although you may need them later). You may just need one or two other people to bounce ideas off. At most, at this stage, you want two or three people from different parts of the company that will be affected by the outcome and one or two experts with the kind of technical know-how you'll need to make the project happen. Choose people you can depend upon to reality check your assumptions, contribute their own ideas to refine and build on yours, answer technical questions, brainstorm with you on ways to proceed, and pitch in with the legwork, research, and analysis you'll need to do during the conceptualization phase. Try to find people who will be able to stick with the project until you meet all your objectives.

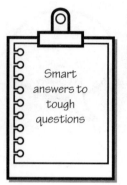

Q: Who should be on your core team?

A: Preferably people as dedicated to the outcome as you are, who can stay the course until the project is complete.

There's another person you'll want with you from the start, your project sponsor. An ideal sponsor is someone one or more levels up the organization from you who is as enthusiastic about this idea as you are and can provide authority for your project team to obtain resources and operate across the organization. Supportive project sponsors assist in the preparation of documentation, advise on decisions that affect the organization across functional lines, and go to bat for the project team when obstacles arise.

First deliverable: your project charter

If this project idea is your brainchild, you are going to have to sell it. But, even if it came from your CEO, you'll need to convince your chief executive and the rest of the organization that you understand it and you're on the right track. So wherever the project idea comes from, your first step is the same. You will need to prepare a project charter that includes, at a minimum:

- Project purpose – which the *PMBOK® Guide* describes as "the business need that the project was undertaken to address."[3]

- Project objectives – the product or service you will create to address the need explained in the project purpose.

- Project sponsor – a key manager who supports the project team.

- Project manager and core team members – a small group that represents those functions that must work together throughout the life of the project.

- Key stakeholders – people whose sign-off you'll need to make this all work.

As well as these, many project charters also include project milestones – interim objectives that must be met *en route* to the final outcome – and a broad preliminary plan for accomplishing the project objectives.

Q: What should my charter contain?

A: Charters vary from one company to the next, so this chapter provides several formats from which to choose.

Smart answers to tough questions

Project charters look different from company to company, but here's an example of an actual one. It comes from AXA Client Solutions in New York. The AXA charter requires only the minimum for initial sign-offs by stakeholders.

PROJECT CHARTER

Project name:

Business Planning Services (for the small-to-middle-market businesses)

Project purpose:

The growth in small and middle-market businesses, the growing scarcity of skilled labor in many markets, and the increased employer demand for enhanced benefits offerings has created an enormous opportunity for financial services companies. Our Diversified Financial "peers" are active in the small-to-middle-business marketplace. However, few offer a coordinated effort and specialize in only a limited number of business offerings while touting a comprehensive service line. In addition, surveys and focus groups of business owners have consistently identified their desire to have comprehensive financial services provided in a coordinated and service-focused manner. AXA Advisors has an opportunity to capitalize on business planning services by leveraging the current infrastructure developed for the individual planning platform and meet the needs of the business market segment.

The small-to-middle-market companies all exhibit a lifecycle from start-up, to growth and maturity, to disposition. Throughout this lifecycle, a business has the need for various products and services ranging from financing, to employee-benefits programs, to tax consulting, to succession planning. The Business Planning Services program would coordinate these offerings with a strong focus on proactive service capabilities.

Business objective:

We have, or are developing, the products, services and e-business resources that our targeted business marketplace needs, within the AXA Financial family of companies and through our alliance relationships. Our business objective is to capitalize on this opportunity by leveraging our existing operations infrastructure and formalizing the "Finder-Minder-Grinder-Binder" concept for the business marketplace. In doing so, we will help meet the company ambition of becoming the leader of wealth management services not only to individual planning clients and non-profits, but also to business owners.

The Business Planning Services Group will be organized around clearly defined functional roles, staffed by individuals hired to do a particular job and supported by experienced planning specialists. Business Planning Services should be introduced in phases to take advantage of products and services that are currently being developed, as well as allow for program enhancements. This program can be piloted without a fee-based version of Business Strategies because a large coordination effort is needed prior to a national introduction.

Business Planning Services provides four major opportunities for AXA Advisors. First, it will help increase revenue for AXA Advisors financial professionals offering financial planning services in the business marketplace. Second, it will give the company the ability to enhance its image as a player in the Diversified Financial arena. Next, the program will attract experienced specialists as recruits from other firms. Finally, it will position our brands in the business owner marketplace and capitalize on their need for a coordinated service-focused offering.

The AXA Advisors brand describes us as trusted advisors and our promise is *Building Futures*. Business Planning Services is consistent with our overall strategy and would provide a greater context and link to the Advanced Practice Models, Paramount Planning Group, and the rest of the retail distribution organization. To compete in the Diversified Financials sector, we need to offer a wider variety of services and focus on the customer service needs to capture a greater portion of the small and middle-market businesses.

Project organization

[Identify the project organization by listing the name, estimated time commitment and phone contact information for the members of the project team.]

Role	Name	Est. Time Commitment	Phone Number
Project Sponsors (Initiative Owners)			
Program Manager (Initiative Manager)			
Business Owner			
Project Leader			
Business Manager			
Development Manager			
Project Manager			

Project signoffs

[The signatures of these key project members define the authority of the project team with regard to the time commitment of the team members, and their staffing assignments in the team organization.]

Name	Signature	Date

Published with permission

Corporate Project Charter
Enter Project Name
Prepared by: Enter Name or Enter Date

Business Issue   Opportunity or problem to address:

                                         Potential risks of not doing the project:

Strategy Alignment   Corporate operating priority that the project supports:

Result Of Work Effort   Deliverables anticipated as a result of the project:

                                           Expected benefits as a result of the project:

Operating Limits/
Interdependencies

Team/ Stakeholders   Project Sponsor:
                                         Project Manager:
                                         Project Team:

                                         Stakeholders:

Project Milestones   High-level timeline for the project, including estimated project start and end dates and completion date of the Solution Definition phase:

Published with permission

What if your management wants even more?

Your organization may expect still more detailed documentation even at this early stage. For example, strategic projects at GlaxoSmithKline in Research Triangle Park, NC, begin with a three-page document, which is reprinted with permission below.

Project Initiation Form

 GlaxoSmithKline

Section 1: Project Definition

Project Name:	Project #:	Sponsor:

Scope Definition	
Concept – Provide background; Identify need; Define outcomes; Determine priorities	**Deliverables** – End product; Work products produced; Establish metrics; Establish how achievement will be measured
Objective – Purpose and Business Strategy links; Goals to be obtained	**Alternatives / Consequences** of not undertaking the project

Benefits	Risks and Issues
Identify; Plan; Assign responsibilities; Track	Identify potential risks; Identify issues and process for resolution

Project Team	Key Customers / Stakeholders
Identify GSK resources required; Define organization and responsibilities; Identify key interfaces and dependencies	Identify key customers of work; Identify key stakeholders; Define their roles and responsibilities

Change Management	Funding Strategy
Define change implications; Identify change strategy and implementation plan; Identify resources required	Source of funds; Disposition of savings; Approvals required; Timing

Sponsor		Date	
Implementation Leader		Date	
OCM Consultant		Date	
Stakeholders		Date	
		Date	
		Date	

Section 1 of 3 Revision 0, 11/28/00

Project Initiation Form

gsk GlaxoSmithKline

Section 2: Implementation Roadmap

	Work / Task Planning				Schedule Planning		
	What needs to be done				When it will be done		
Task Id	Task / Key Activity / Milestone	Task Order	Task Owner	Duration	Start Date	End Date

Overall Timing (Date)

Comments:

Note: Multiple Section 2 pages may be used for larger Work Plans.

OCM Project Management

Revision 0, 11/28/00

Section 2 of 3

Project Initiation Form

Section 3: Finance Management

GlaxoSmithKline

Cost	Acct Code	Current Year				Year 2				Year 3	Year 4	Total
		Q1	Q2	Q3	Q4	Q1	Q2	Q3	Q4	Annual	Annual	Total
GSK Labor												
Travel & Enternment												
Other GSK Labor												
Purchased Labor												
Consultants												
Other Labor Costs												

Labor Subtotal

Other Costs												
Contractor Svcs												
Outside Svcs												
Contingency												

Other Costs Subtotal

Total Target

OCM
Finance

Comments:

Notes: Section 3 is to be completed for costs as well as investments in the business
GSK labor costs include benefits
GSK labor costs will not always be charged to the initiatives
In some cases, the cost/savings will need to be tracked

Section 3 of 3

Revision 0, 11/28/00

Brief or detailed: which way to go

Right now you are probably wishing we told you a project charter must include x, y, and z – no more and no less. Sometimes it's easier to have fewer choices. For better or for worse, the science of project management isn't as rigid as that. Your management may expect a project charter that is as simple as a few paragraphs describing the purpose, objectives, and team. Or it may demand a mini-project plan, complete with assumptions, limits and constraints, cost/benefit analysis, and a draft of the project budget. Or you may need to do both, following the recommendation of some texts on project management, which tell you to:

1   Write a pretty basic charter.

2   Use it to get your project authorized by senior management.

3   Incorporate the more detailed documentation into a Statement of Work. (The trouble is that the label Statement of Work can be confusing, since in many organizations it refers exclusively to work contracted by an outside client.)

If you are not sure what kind of charter will get the most favorable response from upper management in your organization, then:

• Show the examples in this book to your upper management contact and ask for guidance on which way to go.

• Ask someone you know and trust, who has managed successful projects in the past.

• Or, if you are really treading new ground here, go ahead and write a basic charter, then back it up with more details in a separate document. That way you'll be covered for the person who wants only a fast read and for the person who needs to know everything.

Before you start to write

Whether you're aiming for a minimal charter document or a detailed one, don't even start writing until you know:

- *Whose approval you need to move ahead.* Who is going to sanction this project? A high-level management review team? Your boss? Someone, or some group, will have to sign off on this charter to give you the authority to proceed. This is who you are selling yourself to, so keep this audience in mind as you write.

- *Who your sponsor is.* That sounds pretty obvious, because by now you should be convinced that the sponsor is a critical part of the project team. But it's amazing how many project teams try to get started without one – and pay for it later when they run up against obstacles and have no organizational clout to break through them.

  Mike Holveck of GlaxoSmithKline's Office of Change Management, describes attending a meeting of a team that needed a lot of help to meet its deadline. He recalls, "I asked, 'Who is the sponsor?' and I got three different names. One person said it was a committee.

  "I said, 'We really need a sponsor.' They said, 'OK, we'll pick the head of HR.'" But the team was working on an initiative for the sales force. Holveck had to convince them that only someone from the sales force would have the passion and power to provide the support the team needed.

Take Holveck's advice and don't depend upon a committee to be your project's sponsor. There's a Dilbert cartoon captioned, "Be a team player, it diffuses the blame." When it comes to your sponsor, a committee diffuses the responsibility. If the organization has not already assigned your project a highly committed sponsor, go out and find one, someone who shares your passion for the project and is high enough up the ladder to control purse strings and influence other parts of the organization.

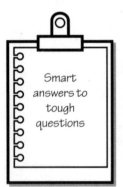

Smart answers to tough questions

Q: Who makes an appropriate sponsor?

A: Someone at a high enough level to make money decisions and have organization-wide influence. At Estée Lauder in Melville, NY, that's usually a site manager. Michael Walker, director of capital budgeting and project management, says his group has steered away from using lower-level managers to fill the sponsor role. Only site managers can make decisions based upon a comparison of all the needs at that site.

- *Who your client is.* "Client? Who's talking about clients?" you might be thinking. It is easy to think about clients if you work for a consulting firm and all your work is project work for outside customers. But if, for example, your project is to improve some internal process that is keeping you and your colleagues from reaching peak performance, you're probably not thinking in terms of a client.

But you have one – or more than one. Your client is whoever you have to satisfy both by the way you do the project work and by the outcome. To identify your client, ask yourself:
  - *Who is going to pay the bills?* The person or organization that wants this project enough to pay for it is certainly a client you will have to satisfy all the way along the line, by sticking to schedule, staying

within budget, and creating a high-quality outcome that meets or exceeds all expectations.

- *Who is going to use the end product?* If your project is to create a new product or service for your company to sell, you have two users to satisfy – your sales and marketing group who have to like it enough to offer it to customers, and the outside customers, who have to like it enough to buy it. You have to satisfy their expectations for cost, quality, and timeliness. If your end product or service never goes outside the walls of your company, which of your colleagues will benefit from it once it is operational? These people are also clients. If you don't meet their needs, they just won't use what you create, all your work will have been in vain, and your hero status will fade fast.

Stakeholder: Anybody and everybody with a "stake" in the project – clients, sponsors, performers, the general public and even the family and friends of direct participants can be considered stakeholders. Not to be confused with the guy that holds the stake when the vampire slayer slays the vampire.

Source: International Institute for Learning, demo of *PM Basics Course* at http://www.iil.com.

- *Who your stakeholders are.* Besides your clients, there are other people who have a stake in what you are doing, people whose lives will change as you implement your project plan or when you finish. Here's a list to get you thinking:
  - *Upper management.* Once they've sanctioned it, they'll have a big stake in the success of your project. If you are working on a strategic priority, you may have to report your progress regularly to a management review team. Their expectations are that you will create a quality output, on time, and within budget.

Smart things to say about managing projects

When you are listing all the people who have a stake in your project, don't forget those who are going to be inconvenienced by it, whose own work won't get done because people are devoting themselves to your project instead.

- *Managers and co-workers of your team members.* A lot of your team members' time is going to go into this project. That's going to change things back in their regular work units where their managers and co-workers will have to make accommodations during the time team members spend on the project.
- *Technical experts you'll call on for crucial parts of the work.* They'll need to schedule their time to meet your needs and the needs of their other ongoing and project work.
- *People who may actually be affected negatively by your success.* If those techies weren't devoted to your project, they'd be working on tasks for someone else, who will be cooling his heels and twiddling his thumbs waiting for his turn. If upper management hadn't funded your project, it might have funded a pet idea of someone else. Now she has to wait until next year to move ahead. And somewhere in the company, there are probably one or two people whose jobs depend upon the continued existence of some process or product the completion of your project will make obsolete. OK, you can't please everyone. But if you can negotiate some peace with these people at the outset, you'll ward off the potential for conflict, if not sabotage, along the way.

Greg Winsper of AXA Client Solutions suggests you ask yourself three questions when you look for stakeholders:

- Who has control to make it not happen?

- Who has the influence to make it not happen?

- Who appreciates it's happening?

Smart answers to tough questions

But what about you? What do you need?

While the project charter is a tangible output of the conceptualization phase of project management, the most important outcome is what you learn about your own project and its context. This is the base you're going to build the project on. So whether your management is satisfied with a bare-bones charter or wants much more information, for your own benefit, be sure you come out of this first phase knowing:

- *The business purpose the project will address.* Make sure you can answer these questions:
  - What strategic initiative will it contribute to? Study the company's strategic plan so you can relate your project to it.
  - What business problem will it solve?
  - What business opportunity will it exploit?
  - What are the business risks of not doing this project?

- *Your project outputs or deliverables.* When the project is finished, what will you have that you didn't have before? In its charters, Northwestern Mutual calls this the "Result of Work Effort." *The PMBOK® Guide* calls it the product description. Whatever you call it, make it very clear. "A better mousetrap" is not specific enough. Exactly what will that mousetrap do that the time-honored set-the-spring and load-the-cheese one doesn't do?

- *The project scope*. What the project will and won't encompass. This covers double territory:
  - *Product specifications*. Requirements you promise your project output will fulfill, such as quality, quantity, performance, reliability, even governmental standards if they apply. To the extent you can, make each attribute measurable. Can you define quality in ISO 9000 terms, for example? How many mousetraps will you be able to produce each year? How many mice can one trap catch in a day? How long will a trap work before it wears out? You won't have all these answers yet, but do your best to develop estimates that you can stand by. If there are attributes your output won't have – e.g., your mousetrap won't catch two mice at once – be clear about those too.
  - *Project objectives*. Not only your output, but your time frame, and your estimated costs (more about that in Chapter 5). If there are issues raised by the business purpose that your project will not address, now is the time to clarify those also.

- *Project constraints*. Here's a really good reason for talking to all the stakeholders before you rush ahead and make promises that will haunt you later. Other people will help you recognize if there are organizational, financial, legal, or other restrictions that will limit what you can do. You need to know now if:
  - *Your budget is going to be much tighter than you hoped*. One thing is for certain. Your budget is not going to be as big as you'd like – budgets never are. If there are budget restrictions in place already, find out what they are and how you can work within them.
  - *The best people for your project are going to be tied up elsewhere*. Identify the people you need and find out their schedules. What will it mean to your project if you have to wait for those people to complete another project or if you have to use someone else altogether.
  - *There is a critical time factor*. If you need to get your product to market before the competition or if someone in the company needs your bril-

liant new process within weeks, you'll be working under a big time constraint that you need to plan for.

- *Your options are limited by contractual obligations.* If your sales office promised the customer mahogany, you can't make those mousetraps out of cedar even if, that way, they would repel moths at the same time.
- *There are laws restricting what you want to do.* If your company has government contracts or is in any kind of environmentally sensitive field – or for a host of other reasons – it may be a good idea to check with your legal department before you surge forward with both guns blazing.

- *Assumptions you are operating under.* Once you have identified the constraints, you are ready to make some assumptions around what you will have going for you. You may have to change these, of course; life is like that. But for now, what assumptions can you reasonably operate under concerning such issues as:
  - *What skills and expertise will be at your command?* Who can you count on being available to do the work you need?
  - *How much money can you expect to get for the project?*
  - *What will that money be able to buy*, in terms of outside resources (inside, too, for that matter, if salaries and equipment costs will come out of your budget)?
  - *By the time your output is ready, what needs will still exist that your product or service will fill?*
  - *What can you leave out because by the time your output is ready that need will have been filled in some other way?*

- *A plan overview* – sometimes called a high-level plan. This doesn't get down to the task level, but it should include the major interim deliverables on your way to your final product or service and a schedule for when you will complete them. For our mousetrap it could include such items as: design approved, raw materials vendors chosen, production facility ready, test product completed, marketing plan completed, promotional materials ready, production begun.

- *Your team.* At this stage you should have lined up a dedicated few who are already working on this with you and have a wish list for a group that, though still small, can oversee all the work that needs to be done.

- *How you are going to communicate* with upper management, your sponsor, stakeholders and team members. You'll do a full-blown communication plan later, but this is the time to start thinking about what reports, meetings, briefing, etc. will keep everyone apprised of your progress and what feedback you'll need to support your actions, especially during the upcoming project planning phase.

Ready to move on

When you've got all that information under your belt, pulled together your core project team, and written up a charter that won sign-offs from stakeholders and upper management giving you the authority to proceed, you are ready to move on to the next phase.

But hang on. That next phase still requires more thinking than acting. It's when the planning really begins.

Smart quotes

Higgins led a 500-person team that had one year to develop a system for BankAmerica to accept deposits across state lines. Everyone was eager to "get to work." But Higgins insisted that the team devote six months to planning the system, evaluating business implications, and anticipating technical challenges – all before it wrote a single line of code. After writing the code, the team spent three months testing and refining it. "My approach is 50% planning, 25% doing, and 25% testing and training. It's a magic formula around here.

Gina Imperato, "He's Become BankAmerica's 'Mr. Project.'" *Fast Company*[4]

The smartest things in this chapter

- The primary deliverable of the Conceptualization Phase is the project charter.

- Depending upon company expectations, a charter can be a few paragraphs or a mini-project plan.

- Before you start writing, identify everyone whose approval you need, your sponsor, your client(s), and all other stakeholders.

- At the end of this phase, you should know your project's purpose, outputs, scope, constraints, assumptions, plan overview, and team members.

Notes

1   Excerpted from *The Little Black Book of Project Management.* Copyright © 1990 by Michael C. Thomsett. Used with the permission of the publisher, AMACOM Books, a division of the American Management Association International, New York, NY. All rights reserved.

2   Excerpted from *Project Management: How to Plan and Manage Successful Projects*, by Joan Knutson, *et al*. Copyright © 1991 AMACOM. Used with the permission of the publisher, AMACOM Books, a division of the American Management Association International, New York, NY. All rights reserved.

3   *A Guide to the Project Management Body of Knowledge*, 1996 ed. Newtown Square, PA: copyright © 1996 Project Management Institute.

4   Quoted from the June 1998 issue of *Fast Company* magazine. All rights reserved.

4

A Carefully Crafted Plan

Let's trace our progress so far. You've got a sign-off on your charter that gives you the authority to proceed. You've got a core team of committed people. Those are the key things you need to proceed to the next project management phase, Planning.

| | Key deliverables | | |
Conceptualization	**Planning**	Delivery	Closure
Project charter. Agreement on the purpose, intended outputs, and scope of the project. Constraints and assumptions you are operating under. Core project team. Commitment of all the stakeholders.	**Project plan including project deliverables, tasks to be done, schedule, assignments, contingency plan, communication plan, and budget.**	Status reports. Project review meetings. Change requests. Updates to project plan, schedule, and budget. Milestones achieved.	All deliverables to fulfill project goals. Final financial accounting. Full documentation of project. Final reports to customers and management. Celebration.

Establishing a baseline

Andrew Gerson, PMP, director of AXA's Project Services Organization in New York and vice-president of the New York City Chapter of the Project Management Institute, refers to project planning as "baselining" the project. A baseline plan covers scope (all the details of the plan with the resources identified), schedule, and cost. (To give costs all the attention they deserve, we are devoting the next chapter exclusively to money.) The term baseline recognizes that the plan will change as the project proceeds, but it gives you a place to start and a direction to follow, standards to measure your progress against, and the ability to assess when you need to make changes and what their impact will be.

What goes into the plan?

Smart things to say

Baseline plan: a plan you work hard to get right the first time so that you can change it regularly as the work progresses.

You don't have to be a newspaper reporter to know the old rules for writing a news lead: Answer the questions *Who? What? Where? When?* and *Why?* You can use almost the same rules for writing a project plan. Just rearrange the prompts a little and substitute *How?* for *Where?*

Your project plan needs to explain Why, What, How, When, and Who.

Project plan

Questions you need to answer	What you need to do	Tools to help you
Why?	If you've done a project charter you've already answered this under Purpose, where you identified the business need your project will address.	Charter
What?	You've got the answer to this one in your charter too, under Objectives or Outputs. Meeting those objectives is *what* your project is intended to do.	Charter
How?	Here's where the new work starts. Your plan needs to spell out how you will reach your objectives. It must include all the deliverables you'll need to produce *en route* to the final outcome and all the tasks necessary to accomplish each deliverable. And to be on the safe side, you'll also have to analyze project risks to anticipate the things that could go wrong and decide how to handle those things if they occur.	Work breakdown structure (WBS) Contingency plan
When?	You'll need a schedule. That's created by sequencing your tasks and determining how long it will take to do each so you can put some dates on your deliverables.	Network diagram Critical path Gantt chart
Who?	Tasks don't just happen. People need to do them, and you'll need to decide who is going to do what based upon their skills and their availability.	Responsibility matrix

Demystifying a project plan

I had a meeting one day with a colleague who said, "Oh, you engineers, all you are going to do is show me a Gantt Chart and focus on the details."

I told her, "What we really need to do is put a plan together."

She replied, "I don't do that very well."

At a dry erase board, I said, "Let's do a to-do list." She rattled off all the things we needed to do. I wrote them on the board.

When we were finished, I said, "Let's talk about sequence. Is this the right order?"

"Pretty much," she answered. I think we changed maybe one or two things.

I said, "OK, let's look at these, and you tell me how long you think it will take to do each. She replied a day for this, maybe a week for that.

When we were finished, I told her, "You just did a project plan. You told me you couldn't, but you did. You had it all in your head. You're probably just not used to putting it in the kind of format engineering people put it in. By putting it in this format, we're able to communicate your plan to others. That's why we do this."

Now we're close friends and we talk about that day often. We gave her a hard-hat and pocket protector and told her, "Now you are an honorary engineer."

Michael Holveck, GlaxoSmithKline

Paula K. Martin and Karen Tate are columnists for *PM Network*, the PMI magazine, co-authors of the *Project Management Memory Jogger™* – a step-by-step guide to managing a project, and the forces behind one of the most practical and entertaining project management sites on the Internet, www.projectresults.com. You can download a generic project plan template and a preview of their *Memory Jogger* that by itself provides a clear map of the project management process. You can even begin to read a medieval project management mystery novel or send a question to its heroine, who will provide down-to-earth answers expressed with 21st century sassiness. Martin and Tate will make you laugh and learn.

SMART PEOPLE TO HAVE ON YOUR SIDE:

PAULA K. MARTIN AND KAREN TATE

Where to start

Since we're assuming you have your charter, explaining what you are going to do and why, your first step now is to determine how. To achieve that, call your team together and create a work breakdown structure (WBS).

Q: What if the team questions the purpose and objectives that have already been signed off on in the charter?

A: Nothing is set in stone until the project is over. You may hear some really important ideas that are well worth bringing to the attention of your sponsor and senior management. On the other hand, don't be swayed by whoever speaks the loudest and longest. It's your judgment to make. That's what project managers get the big bucks for.

Smart answers to tough questions

The WBS is the engine that drives the project. From it, you create your schedule, determine resource requirements, develop a budget, and make assignments. Without it, your project would flounder in chaos.

In its simplest form, a WBS is what management consultant Rosalind Gold of New York calls "a super to-do list." You could write your WBS as a messy list on the back of an envelope – and that's just about what managers of small projects often do. But you'd probably lose it before you could use it to manage or control anything, so it's a good idea to get familiar with some standard formats that survive better and can be clearly understood by others.

A WBS contains all the tasks that have to be done to complete the project, organized into categories. You can create one in either outline or chart form, usually displayed in levels with major deliverables at the higher levels and detailed tasks at the lowest levels.

Imagine, if you will, that you have agreed to manage a class reunion dinner project. Simple as that sounds, it will allow us to illustrate the WBS and other project management tools that you'd use for building a bridge or launching a new marketing program.

If you were managing that dinner project, your top level might include such items as participation, site, program, and materials. At the next level you'd list the tasks included under each category.

Written as an outline, the WBS for the reunion dinner could look like this:

Class reunion dinner

1 Participation
    1.1 Obtain class list
    1.2 Send invitations
    1.3 Finalize attendee list

2 Site

2.1 Visit potential sites

2.2 Contract with site

2.3 Choose menu

3 Program

3.1 Create agenda

    3.1.1 Choose chairperson

    3.1.2 Choose speakers

3.2 Arrange entertainment

    3.2.1 Identify potential entertainers

    3.2.2 Contract with entertainer

4 Materials

4.1 Identify potential printers

4.2 Select printer

4.3 Print invitations

4.4 Souvenir program

    4.4.1 Write souvenir program

    4.4.2 Print souvenir program

If lists with numbers like 3.2.1 make your eyes glaze over, then you might prefer a work breakdown structure that looks like Fig. 4.1.

Starting with major deliverables and working downward is what project management specialists call "decomposition." The number of levels into which you decompose your WBS depends upon the complexity of your project. To stage a smashing farewell party for a departing colleague, you could probably get by with one or two levels handwritten on the back of an envelope. To build a world class business-to-business website, you'll need multiple levels that could fill a book (although to keep your sanity, you'd probably stop after a few levels, creating subprojects that would each require its own WBS).

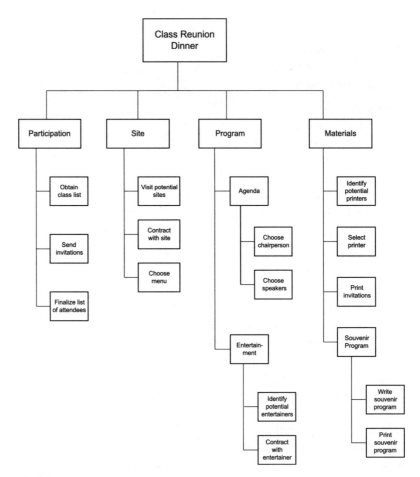

Fig. 4.1

For a large project, you may want to break your WBS into sequential stages. You could choose to organize a project for building a new office, for example, into stages such as design, contracting, building, decorating, landscaping, and moving in. With this kind of WBS, it is only the first stage that needs to be decomposed to the task level at this time. You can stick with higher levels for subsequent stages until the time approaches to begin work on them.

Whether it's simple or complex, creating a WBS is seldom a one-person job. It's usually a task for the project manager and the core team, who begin by brainstorming all the project requirements and the tasks required to achieve them. With a flipchart pad and multiple colored sticky notes, you can arrange all your brainstormed ideas into what Sunny and Kim Baker (authors of *The Complete Idiot's Guide to Project Management*) call an "organization chart for the project."[1]

Q: In a WBS, how big a unit of work is a task?

A: To some degree that's a judgment call. You aren't going to decompose "send invitations" into address envelopes and lick stamps. On the other end of the spectrum was the to-do list of a salesman in an old cartoon. It said: Prospect, Sell, Retire.

One guideline is the 8/80 rule described by Sunny and Kim Baker in *The Complete Idiot's Guide to Project Management*: Keep your tasks between 8 hours (one work day) and 80 hours (ten work days).[2]

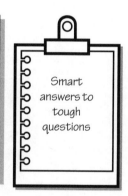

Smart answers to tough questions

When you think the WBS is complete, take Rosalind Gold's advice and mentally walk through your list to ensure nothing is missing. Does successful completion of the tasks lead inevitably to the objective? If you and your core team are not sure of all the tasks, get some input from experts in each of the categories.

When you *know* the WBS is complete, you've got the information you need to develop a schedule, assign tasks, and begin to develop a budget for the project.

Don't reinvent the wheel

The good news about work breakdown structures is that you shouldn't have to create a new one from scratch every time you begin a new project. Every project is indeed unique, but not in every respect. If you save your class reunion dinner WBS, it can serve as a generic WBS for the next reunion. And with a little tweaking, you could use it for masterminding a community awards dinner or the Girl Scouts father/daughter bash.

Many organizations are developing generic WBSs for various types of projects. (In fact, many companies have project management offices that, among other things, serve as repositories for the historical files from all company projects. If your organization has such a function, run, don't walk, to find out what it has on file and how it can help.) Since by definition your project is different from what the organization has done before, a generic WBS may not fit exactly, but it can give you a great leg up on planning. If your organization isn't collecting these, why don't you take responsibility for beginning such a collection with the WBS for your next project?

Sequencing the tasks

Inexperienced project managers tend to leap right from the work breakdown structure to developing a work schedule, which suddenly turns into an abyss. Unless the project is really simple, they find themselves spiraling out of control, trying to figure out which tasks to do first. Project management depends upon another tool for solving that: the network diagram. If the work breakdown structure is the engine driving your project, the network diagram is your map to follow. Just as you couldn't schedule your arrival at grandma's house if you didn't know how far away it was and what route to take, you can't schedule your project until you've plotted your network diagram.

Using boxes connected by arrows, the network diagram sequences all tasks from left to right chronologically, showing at a glance which tasks have to be done before another one can be started, which can be done concurrently, and which are independent of each other. In project management terminology:

Smart things
to say

Network diagram: a map of
the project.

- A task that must be completed before another can be started is said to have *precedence* over the other.

- A task that cannot be started until another is completed is *dependent* upon the first one.

- Diagramming these precedences and dependencies shows the *logical relationships* between project tasks, which is why network diagrams are often called logic diagrams.

A network diagram:

- *Lays out the path that leads inexorably toward your goal.* Without this, you are bound to find yourself locked in a Catch-22 situation where you can't do Step C because you didn't do Step B. But you couldn't do Step B because it required output from Step D, which couldn't be done before C ... well, you get the picture. As you create the network diagram, you work out these sticky chicken and egg questions.

- *Identifies dependencies between tasks in different parts of the work breakdown structure.* For our class reunion dinner, for example, we can't finalize our headcount for the site until we've finalized our attendee list and we can't write our souvenir program until we've completed the agenda and arranged for the entertainment.

- *Illustrates which tasks are independent of each other and can be done concurrently* – and if two independent tasks both have to be done before you can begin a third task down the road.

- *Prepares you to create a schedule.* When you know the order in which tasks have to be done, you can start to put them on a calendar.

- *Helps you discover gaps in your WBS.* In fact, a network diagram acts like another check on the WBS. If you discover there's no way to get from point A to point B, there must be some missing steps. In the network diagram for the class reunion dinner that follows, you'll notice one step we hadn't anticipated when we created the work breakdown structure: give the restaurant a final headcount five days before the event.

For a simple project, you can probably lay out your diagram on a single page. But for a complex project, you may want to start with an overview network diagram, plotting the relationships between project milestones. When you fill in the tasks leading up to each milestone, you can expect to fill a book – or better yet, a wall or two. Posting your diagram makes it easy for the whole team to review it together.

SMART VOICES

> Project management consultant Marie Scotto of The Scotto Group in New York City says the best project team meetings take place with everybody standing around a large posted network diagram, rather than sitting around a conference table each studying his or her own page and asking, "Wait a minute, what task are we on?"

There are various conventions for drawing network diagrams. Probably the simplest is to:

- put tasks into boxes;

- connect boxes from left to right with arrows pointing from tasks that must be done first to tasks that depend upon them; and

- put tasks that can be done concurrently in a vertical column, with no connection arrows between them.

Drawn that way, a network diagram for our reunion dinner would look like the one in Fig. 4.2.

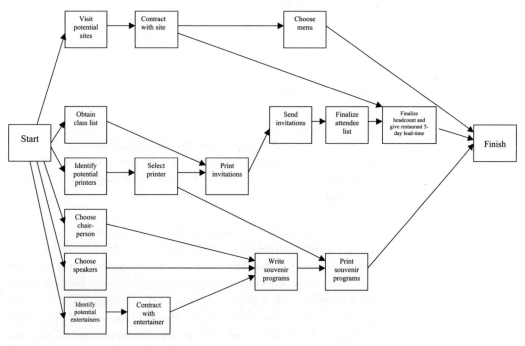

Fig. 4.2

This method of diagramming seems natural for anyone who's ever created or read a flow chart, but you may encounter variations on it. One variation is a diagram made up of circles and arrows, with the circles numbered to represent the tasks. The diagram takes up less space that way, but you'll need a legend to identify the tasks by number, so the diagram is harder to follow. And it's less dramatic. It's difficult to imagine a project team standing around that kind of network diagram and getting excited about it.

Some people even put the tasks on the arrows and the dependencies in the nodes (circles or squares). For most of us, that seems less intuitive, but it works for some applications.

Whichever method you use, here are some tips for making it accurate and complete:

1   Think it through first. For each task, ask yourself:

    • What tasks do we have to do before we can do this one?
    • What tasks can't be done until this one is completed?
    • Are these real dependencies or just the way we've always done things? This is an easy trap to fall into and a waste of good project management techniques.

2   Expect to make a lot of changes as you go along. So gather plenty of sharp pencils and a couple of good erasers. Or write all the tasks on colored sticky notes so you can move them around on big flip chart pages until you get the order just right. Or you can plot your network diagram on a computer, using project management software, but it won't do your thinking for you. The computer doesn't know you can't print your invitations until you've selected a printer. Whatever method you use, as you proceed, you'll discover missing tasks, dependencies you hadn't thought of before, maybe even unnecessary tasks. If a task turns out to have no dependencies, ask yourself if you have to do it at all.

3 Involve your team. This isn't a one-person task. Others will spot relationships and shortcuts you may not know about.

4 Check it by working it backward. Start at the end and ask yourself at each step: what has to be done before we do this? Some people actually build the network from end to beginning the first time around. If you are one of those, then check it by working forward.

5 Don't file it away. Post it and use it. It's not an historical document, it's a map, and like any road map it can change as roadblocks occur, detours pop up, and new superhighways get built. It's also a vivid illustration of the complexity of the project. Scotto tells a story of a beleaguered project team under pressure to hurry a complex project. One day the company president joined the team as it clustered around its network diagram wall. Then he asked for a full-sized copy of the diagram. "I'm going to take it up to [my boss]," he said, "and ask him, 'Tell me what to leave out.'"

How long is all this going to take?

Even when you know the project is going to end on March 31 (because that's your manuscript deadline and the publisher has fixed it by putting the book in the fall catalog), you still need to figure out how much time each of your tasks is going to take so you can schedule them to make that final deadline happen. In project management terminology, the time required to complete an activity is referred to as its *duration*.

There is more than one way to determine duration of tasks. One of the fanciest ways to calculate duration is using PERT (Program Evaluation and Review Technique). Although the acronym has been co-opted to mean any network diagram – much like any tissues are called Kleenexes – a PERT

Chart is really a specialized network diagram that incorporates durations based on a formula that combines a weighted mix of three time estimates: most optimistic, most likely, and most pessimistic. It's unlikely that you'll ever be expected to do a real PERT calculation, but knowing about it is a good reminder to bear those three possibilities in mind as you do your time estimates.

Most people probably use their good judgment when it comes to estimating durations. You can do that as long as you base your judgment upon all the information and advice you can get. Ask people who have done such work in the past. Find out from industry associations what the standards are, if any, for this work. Think about the resources you'll have access to: will they speed up the task or slow it down? If there is any waiting time enforced between tasks, build it into the duration of the earlier task. This is illustrated in the class reunion dinner project with the task, "finalize headcount and give restaurant five-day lead time."

Consider all these things, and run your best guesses by the team for their input. And when you've come up with a number, ask yourself if you have really given enough consideration to that PERT component: most pessimistic. Do you need to add a little more time just in case? Some people call that padding; others call it being realistic. Marie Scotto calls it contingency and says the most important place to add it is at the end, building in extra time between scheduled completion and delivery. (In the case of our reunion, delivery would be the gala event itself.) If dates slip along the way, that's where push finally comes to shove and you need the extra time to survive.

Adding it up

Now you've estimated the duration for each task, but with those tasks spread all over your labyrinth of a network diagram, how do you add up the times to figure out how long the entire project will take? Obviously you are not going to add up the durations of all the tasks; some of them will happen concurrently. Instead you are going to sum up the times required only by those tasks on what is called the *critical path*. The critical path determines the least amount of time in which you can complete the project by tracing the longest route through the network diagram.

Smart things
to say

Critical path: the longest distance between two points – the starting point and the end point.

Here's the quick and dirty way to find the critical path. First write all the task durations into the task boxes in your network diagram. Now think of the lines on the diagram as roads, and you'll see that there appear to be various roads that go from start to finish. Add up the durations of tasks along each of these alternate roads. The longest road is the critical path. Think about it: This is actually the least amount of time the project can take. Everything not on the critical path can be done concurrently. But if you said to yourself, "I'll reduce my time by taking one of the shorter paths," it wouldn't work, because you wouldn't have time to do things on the critical path.

If we used that method to find the critical path to our reunion dinner, the result would look like Fig. 4.3, which has durations in days inserted into each task box and the critical path outlined in bold. Adding the task durations along the critical path, the minimum duration for the entire project is 49 days.

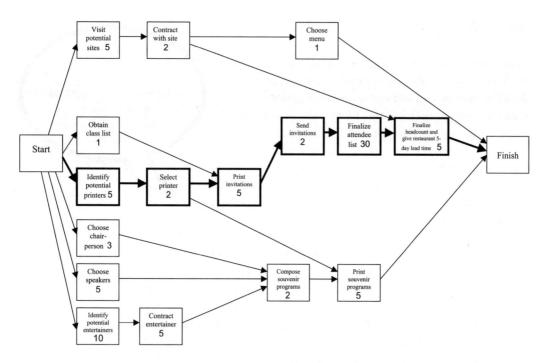

Fig. 4.3   Network diagram showing task durations, with critical path indicated in bold.

Now here's the official way to find the critical path. You may not need to do this, at least not without project management software to relieve you of the onerous drawing and calculations, but in the world of project management you are going to hear people using the terms involved here, so it's a good idea to know what they mean.

1   Determine the *early start and finish dates* for each task on the network diagram. Those are the earliest possible dates to begin and end each task. To calculate them, take a *forward pass* through the network diagram, i.e. move through it from left to right.

- Start with the first task. The early start date for the first task is Day 0.
- The early finish date for the first task is Day 0 plus its duration. For example, one of the first tasks for the class reunion dinner is Identify potential printers. The earliest start date is 0 and the duration is 5 days so the early finish date is 5.
- The early finish date of one task is the early start date of the next. If a task is dependent upon two or more tasks that precede it, look for the *latest* early finish date among the tasks with precedence. Use that number as the early start date of the dependent task. (You can't begin that task until all the tasks with precedence are completed.) Proceed through the network diagram calculating each early start and finish date this way.

Fig. 4.4 shows the result of a forward pass through the center layer of the class reunion dinner network diagram.

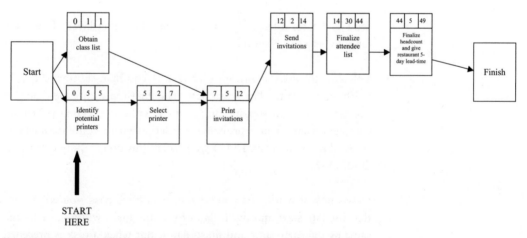

Fig. 4.4 Forward pass for early start and finish dates. Early start is in the top left corner of each task box. Early finish is in the top right corner. The duration is top center.

2   Determine the *late start and finish dates* for each task. These are the latest possible dates to begin and end each task and still get the project done on schedule. To do that, take a *backward pass* through the network diagram, i.e. move through it from right to left.

- Start with the last task. You need a finish date to begin the process, so use the one you just identified, i.e. take your early finish date for that task and use it as the late finish date.
- Subtract the duration for the task to determine its late start date.
- Move left on the network diagram to the preceding task. The late finish date for that task is the same as the late start date for task to the right of it on the diagram. Proceed through the network diagram from end to beginning calculating each start and finish date this way.

See Fig. 4.5 for a backward pass through the center layer of the class reunion network diagram.

3   Calculate the *float*, if any, for each task. To do that, subtract the early finish date from the late finish date. The float represents the time you can get away with slipping on that task without affecting your final completion date. You're probably wondering where we got the idea you could slip on any task. Didn't we base all this on carefully calculated durations?

Here's how it works. As you do your backward pass, you will notice that the late start and finish dates for many tasks will be exactly the same as the early start and finish dates. But when a task is preceded by two others and they have different durations, then the one with the shortest duration is going to be lucky enough to have some float time.

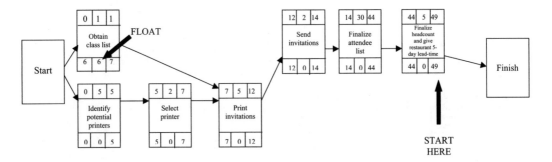

Fig. 4.5 Backward pass for late start and finish dates. Late start is in the bottom left of each task box. Late finish is bottom right. Float is bottom center.

On Figure 4.5, you can see that only the task, Obtain class list, has float. (If you worked a forward and backward pass through all the other tasks on the entire network diagram shown in Figure 4.3, you would find that they also have float.)

4 Trace the critical path. Calculated this way, the critical path is the route through the tasks that have no float. There is no float anywhere on the critical path. Early start and finish dates are the same as late start and finish dates. What that means is that any time you miss a deadline on a task along the critical path you will have an impact on the final completion date.

Figure 4.6 shows the critical path for our class reunion dinner project, calculated by this method. If you compare it with Fig. 4.3, you will see that the critical path is the same on both.

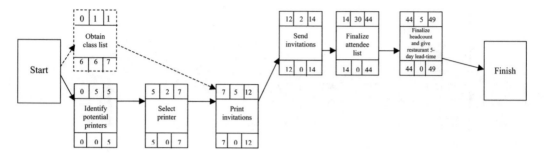

Fig. 4.6 The critical path. All task boxes and arrows made of solid lines are along the critical path.

Critical path, one more time

This is a really important concept in project management planning. Not only does it remind you when you are in danger of blowing your deadline unless you take corrective action, the critical path also tells you where you need to pile on people, money, and other resources if you are forced to make choices between fully supporting one task or another at a particular point in time.

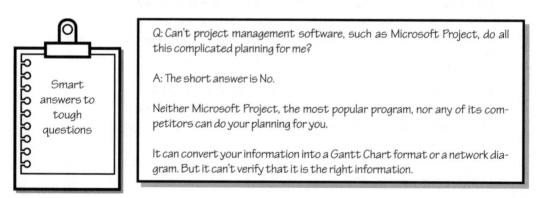

Smart answers to tough questions

Q: Can't project management software, such as Microsoft Project, do all this complicated planning for me?

A: The short answer is No.

Neither Microsoft Project, the most popular program, nor any of its competitors can do your planning for you.

It can convert your information into a Gantt Chart format or a network diagram. But it can't verify that it is the right information.

It can locate a critical path, but only after you have determined the dependencies and task durations.

It can create links to all the relevant data stored in other programs on your computer or network, but it can't create the data or decide what's relevant to what.

It can keep track who is doing what, but it can't decide who should do what.

It can tell you if you are overspending your budget, but it can't decide how much you should be spending.

It can generate a wide variety of reports, but it can only use the information you feed into it.

Q. Does that mean project management software is not worth using?

A. Oh no, not at all. All the things listed above that the software can do are valuable reasons for using it. And they are only the beginning. Used properly it can help you:

- Schedule tasks and organize resources.
- Exchange information over an intranet or the Internet with team members and other stakeholders.
- See the impact of any planned change. Input a change into one screen and the software carries it through your entire plan. It won't let you, for example, change an expenditure in one place, but forget to calculate the impact of that expenditure somewhere else.
- Make decisions based on what/if scenarios. You can plug in alternatives and see what the impacts are.

There's a tremendous amount that project management software can do to ease the mechanical aspects of planning and tracking progress. But it can't think and it can't do the project work. Many a project leader has gotten into trouble by forgetting that.

So, to recap, the characteristics of the critical path are:

- It is the longest path from start to finish.

- It tells us the minimum time for the entire project.

- Tasks on the critical path have no float (or slack time).

- Any delay in completing any task along the critical path will delay the completion of the entire project.

Finally, the schedule

By translating duration of each task into calendar dates, you create a schedule. Of course, it's not that simple. Even as you develop the schedule, you will discover some needs to adjust it. Perhaps the people or equipment required to do a task are only available at certain times. What if a holiday interrupts your schedule? Using our class reunion dinner as an example, what if now, for the first time, you notice that your five days for printing invitations fall over a weekend? Suddenly your critical path is out of whack. You've got decisions to make. Can you change the date for the dinner? Can you start working on it sooner? Can you afford to pay for a rush print job? Better to solve these problems now than discover them at the last minute when it's too late to adjust.

When you've smoothed out the bumps in the schedule, a good way to display it is using everyone's favorite method: the Gantt Chart.

Remember our road trip analogy, with the WBS as engine and network diagram as road map. Similarly, you can think of a Gantt Chart as your project's itinerary. It is a graphic display of where you need to be at any point in your project timeline if you are going to reach your destination on time.

Gantt Charts are popular because they are easy to create (once you've done the upfront WBS and network diagram), easy to read, and dramatic for comparing actual with planned times for tracking progress. Any project-management software worth its bytes will produce an eye-catching, brightly colored chart – or several if you break a long project into chunks that your eyes and brain can comprehend at a glance. Or you can draw your own with a pen, a ruler and some colored markers.

> Smart things to say
>
> Gantt Chart: a format for laying out the project schedule, showing beginning and end dates for each activity.

A Gantt Chart is simply a bar chart with activities listed down the left side and dates along the top. Date-placed horizontal bars show the sequence and beginning-to-end time of each activity. If you create one with space for both projected and actual schedules, you can fill in the actual as you go along, producing a vivid illustration of how well you are meeting your schedule. When the plan bars and the real-life bars fall out of sync, you know you'd better change the plan or the way you are implementing it.

A Gantt Chart for our class reunion dinner, to be held on May 30, could look like Fig. 4.7, assuming we didn't discover any weekend hitches. (This displays only those tasks on the partial network diagram we used for estimating early and late start and finish dates.)

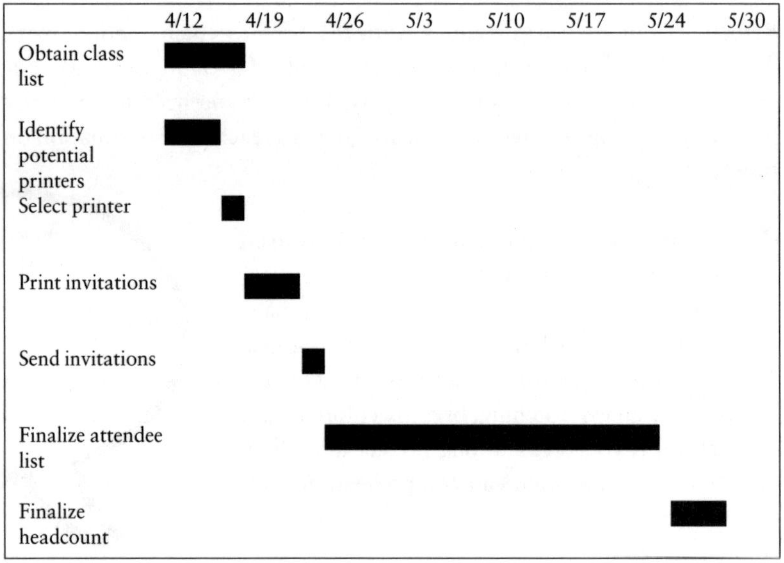

Figure 4.7 A Gantt Chart for our class reunion dinner

Next question: who is going to do each task?

In fact, this isn't really the *next* question. It is one you should be working on concurrently with your schedule.

One otherwise sensible book on project management insists you must assign people to tasks based only on skills, never on availability. The only reasonable response to that seems to be, "Get real." If you had that much power to command the universe, you wouldn't have had to worry about constraints when you were conceptualizing the project. You could just order up what you wanted and demand, "Make it so."

But even in the real world, this doesn't mean you shouldn't beg, cajole, pull strings, even bribe to get the people you know will do the best job on key tasks. It does mean, however, that there will be times when you will have to settle for whoever is available if you are locked into a set schedule or a fixed budget. Andrew Gerson of AXA stresses that planning is all about trade-offs among scope (project requirements), schedule, and cost.

For assigning project team members to tasks, be sure to consider:

- who has the best skills for the task;

- who wants to do it;

- who is available to do it; and

- who works well with the other people assigned to the same or interdependent tasks.

If you have to search outside the team for talent, you'll need to:

- *Look in-house to see if the talent is available.* If you and your team don't know the good people, check with functional management, enlist your sponsor's help, and ask around among people you trust.

- *Be prepared to negotiate for the selected person's time.* The more specific you can be – and, of course, the more flexible you can be – the better response you are likely to get from both your functional expert and her manager.

- *Go to an outside vendor if necessary.* If you do that, be absolutely certain about the skills you need and the precise work the person will do. Be sure to get good references, preferably from someone you know, and a guarantee. You can get the talent you want when you want it this way if you are willing to pay the price.

Making task assignments is another job best done with the input of the entire project team. You'll learn about skills you didn't even know people had that way, and you'll learn about absolute aversions to doing certain work. Most people will pitch in and do what's necessary whether they enjoy it or not when they recognize the need and make their own decision to do so. But told to perform against their will, they'll resist either actively or passively in a way that could cost your success. You'll get buy-in when assignments are a team decision.

Keeping track of who is doing what

As you may have guessed, project-management practitioners have a favorite format for displaying task assignments. It's called the responsibility assignment matrix.

Smart things to say

Responsibility assignment matrix: a graphic representation of who is going to do what.

The responsibility assignment matrix lists tasks down one side and people along the top, designating responsibilities under each name. For a simple project, the designation may be a checkmark. For more complicated ones, you may need to differentiate among various levels of involvement with keys like A for accountable, P for participant, R for review, and S for sign-off.

Using the tasks on our class reunion dinner Gantt Chart to demonstrate, here's what the project's responsibility assignment matrix might look like. Let's assume the team members are Evelyn, Kim, and Juan.

Task	Evelyn	Kim	Juan
Obtain class list	A		
Identify potential printers		A	P
Select printer		A	
Print invitations		A	
Finalize attendee list	P		A
Finalize headcount	A		

Posted on the wall where everyone can see it or available online for teams whose members are far flung, the responsibility assignment matrix is an easy way for everyone to see who is responsible for what and who is helping whom.

It takes more than people

To do their jobs well, people need tools and equipment. Now's the time to sit down with each person assigned to a task and identify what those needs are. Some of what you get will be a wish list, some of it crucial. Between you and each person, you'll need to figure out which is which.

Distributing resources

We've talked about availability and we've alluded to budget constraints, but we haven't really faced the real-life problem you are going to confront. There are simply never enough resources – people, money, and sometimes equipment – to go around. It happens even on enviable projects that have the blessing of the CEO and the budget to go with it.

Kathleen Warren, vice president of Gartner, the Stanford, Connecticut-based technology services firm, found that out when she took over a semi-stalled project to create a corporate alumni program – later named Gartner Alumni Connect. The project had the sponsorship of the CEO, who conceived of it as a way to showcase Gartner to previous employees and build them into a network of goodwill ambassadors for the company. At its heart would be an alumni Web site, and therein lay the rub. At the very same time, a much larger Gartner project team was in the process of building a new corporate Web site intended to spearhead a business transformation for the company, providing its clients with vastly increased access to online services. What that meant for Warren was that there just weren't any in-house people with Web skills left to work on her project.

She wasn't left entirely on her own. Julie Viscardi, who reported to the head of human resources, sized up the situation and asked her boss to free her up to help Warren. "What started as 'I'll help you as much as I can,' became full-time as we got to launch date," Viscardi recalls. Warren delegated to her such tasks as site testing, resolving data privacy issues, and database management. That allowed Warren to focus on getting the site launched and making sure the content was appropriate to the audience.

Warren and Viscardi pulled off an award-winning result, on time and within budget, but they had to leverage their own time carefully (which admittedly often meant working extremely long hours) and go to outside sources for the technical talent they needed. What that led to is the heart of a story you'll come to later in this chapter when you get to the section on analyzing risk.

Back to more typical projects: they don't usually have the direct involvement of the CEO and the budget is often tight. Where does that leave you when you realize you have XX number of tasks to get done and only X number of people and dollars to spread among them? Ask yourself these questions:

- *Can I move resources from non-critical path activities to critical path activities?* This is one reason it's essential to identify the critical path. If a task doesn't need to be done for two weeks, the people and equipment you planned to assign to it may be able to spend the first week helping out on a more pressing critical path activity.

- *Can I bargain for more resources?* If your budget is locked up tight, all you have to offer may be your good will. When you go back to the line managers and beg again for more people and borrowed equipment, it helps if you've built a network of contacts you've done favors for or otherwise built good relationships with in the past. It's not a bad idea to make an early list of everyone in the organization who holds you and your team members in high regard.

- *Could we alter the scope without significantly reducing the end result?* What if we skipped the printed programs for our reunion dinner, for example? That would eliminate a task and a budget item. Would it spoil the evening for our classmates?

- *Could we find a less expensive alternative to one of our deliverables?* What if we forgot about hiring an entertainer and persuaded those guys who had a band back in high school to regroup and perform for us at the reunion dinner?

- *Could we change the schedule?* Is the final delivery date set in stone or is it discretionary? If we pushed it back a month, would that ease the problem of not having enough people to complete the task?

- *If none of these would work, could we downsize the scope?* What if, for example, we changed our dinner to a lunch?

Solving resource problems requires making trade-offs among scope, budget, and schedule and trading on your good will.

But what if …

What if my best programmer quits? What if my only team member who can charm the tech support people into putting us at the top of their schedule gets sick? And what if, while she's sick, the system crashes? What if there is a fire in our warehouse and all our supplies get destroyed? What if there is a tidal wave …

Enough already!

Actually those questions are not all the mutterings of a pessimistic worrywart or the ramblings of a paranoid schizophrenic. Every project carries with it the risk of unexpected events that can delay it, cripple it, or even kill it. The solution is to deliver those events out of the realm of unexpected and into the category of anticipated so you are prepared to manage them if they occur.

To do that, you and your team need to name those risks and look them squarely in the face. The most common method is to get the team together and brainstorm all the "what ifs" you can come up with. To get you started here's a general list of risks that hover over almost any project:

"The most common error in planning is to assume that there will be no errors in the implementation."

Gerard M. Blair, *Planning a Project*, http://www.ee.ed.ac.uk/~gerard/Management/art8.html

- *It may cost more than you think.* Rising energy costs, wage increases, changes in vendors, higher costs of raw materials – any one of these could boost your costs. Are you prepared for them?

- *It may require expertise you don't have.* What if you can't find people with the skills you need when you need them? What if people you are depending upon leave?

- *It may take longer than you anticipate.* If, for example, you can't find skilled people and you have to train someone, what will that do to your schedule?

- *It may have an undesirable effect on another part of the business.* If your great idea is going to undermine someone else's job, you may be confronting a powerful lobby resisting your every move.

- *It may be torpedoed by changing technology or customer whims.* Remember the old story about the company that made the world's greatest buggy whip just in time for cars to arrive on the scene. Technology changes so fast these days that almost every idea risks becoming a buggy whip before it gets off the ground.

- *It may end up the victim of a political upheaval in your organization.* In some companies, top management changes as fast as technology.

- *Vendors may not provide exactly what you expect.* Through misunderstandings, mismanagement of risks on their part, or – dare we say it – occasional deceit, vendors don't always come through with what you need when you need it.

When you brainstorm your list, you'll undoubtedly come up with additional ones unique to your project. For example, for their Business Planning

Services Project (whose charter you read in Chapter 3), the AXA Client Solutions project team acknowledged this list of risks:

- lack of resources to coordinate and bring together all facets of the company;

- lack of customer service in "minding" the relationships;

- systems limitations in implementing new compensation structure;

- ignoring client focus and evaluating needs of the business owner; and

- inability to communicate a team "value proposition."

Some of the items on your list will be imminent dangers; others may seem far-fetched. For example, in most parts of the world, a tidal wave is probably not something you need to plan for. But if your boiler has been springing leaks and flooding the basement storage every few months, maybe you'd better look for another place to store your records.

To qualify risks as worthy of attention, start by estimating the probability of their occurring. Rate each one high, medium, or low. Then rate the potential impact of the risk, should it occur, in the same way. It's pretty obvious what to do about the ones that rate high/high: Attend to them now. Those that rate low/low can go at the bottom of your priority list of things to worry about. The high/medium combinations deserve your attention. For anything with one low rating, ask yourself:

- How much effort or money would it take to cover this risk? Is it worth it?

- Can we buy insurance to cover it?

- If this risk were to occur, would there be a company left to worry about?

What to do

When you've made up your mind which risks you are going to worry about, you still need to decide what to about them. The *PMBOK® Guide* provides three categories of response:

- Avoidance – eliminating the cause of the risk.

- Mitigation – reducing the probability of the risk occurring or the cost if it does.

- Acceptance – acknowledging that the risk event may occur, and developing a contingency plan to deal with it when it does.

Obviously, avoidance is ideal, but not always possible. If the vendor you favor for his highly creative work has a track record of missed deadlines, you can use a different vendor instead. Unless, of course, the only other vendor in town costs twice as much, putting her outside your budget.

You may be able to mitigate the probability of equipment failure by buying or leasing a better brand. Or you might mitigate the cost of equipment failure by obtaining a service contract.

Smart things to say

Contingency plan: an alternate series of steps to take when Murphy's Law strikes.

But many of your risks will fall into the acceptance category, and for those you need contingency plans. If you recognize in advance that the workload on one task may overwhelm the people assigned to it, you'll have a better idea whom you can pull off another activity at each point in time. If you acknowledge that your system may have some bugs in it, you can have people ready to troubleshoot them. If you admit to yourself early that you may have a cost overrun, you can probably lower it even if you can't eliminate it.

www.Gartner-alumni.com, an online meeting place for past employees of Gartner, the technology services firm, was launched on time and within budget to overwhelmingly positive response. Vice President Kathleen Warren, project manager; Julie Viscardi, who volunteered to join the project; and Kevin Volpe, technical troubleshooter par excellence, won a coveted Silver Award for their efforts. Warren received the prestigious Gold Award from the CEO and was promoted. Viscardi moved into a new job she loves, managing the alumni project full-time.

What could be better than that?

Well, Viscardi admits, the project was not without its trials. Still, all's well that ends well. Especially if you learn from your experiences.

What she learned, Viscardi is quick to reveal, is the importance of managing risks.

You could say the project fell to Warren in the first place as a result of a risk fulfilled. The first project manager quit the company suddenly only months before the announced launch date. Furthermore, when Warren and Viscardi got on board, they discovered the project was not nearly as far along as anybody thought. In fact they were starting from scratch. They mitigated that problem with hard work and long hours. They also leveraged Warren's 12-year tenure with the company to take advantage of her network of in-house colleagues and former colleagues who had moved on. That helped them get the massive amount of information they needed to ensure the program would meet users' needs.

But the real crunch came a week before the scheduled launch date, when Warren and Viscardi discovered bugs in the program. The "tangled web of vendors," as Viscardi describes them, blamed each other. The problems at that stage weren't big – one was with the time/date stamp – but they were enough that the team could imagine site visitors snorting, "Gee, they gave us something and it doesn't even work." That kind of reaction wasn't going to contribute to the community of good will the project was created to develop.

First corrective step: Delay the launch one week. They could do that and stay within the promised time frame. That let them buy a little time.

But, says Viscardi, a big problem was that she and Warren just couldn't communicate with the vendors in the technical language necessary to get a grip on the issues. Unfortunately for them, all the people at Gartner with the right expertise were working on creating the new corporate Web site. So, Viscardi recalls, "I went to the CIO and begged for help."

And help she got. The CIO lent the project his best troubleshooter, Kevin Volpe, whose regular job was managing the group that solves clients' technical problems, not internal ones. After Gartner's head of networking figured out the problem the Friday before the new Monday launch date, Volpe and his group worked round the clock over the weekend to fix the site.

The site launched that Monday, looking great to visitors. But for the Gartner team the problems hadn't ended. With Warren now off on sabbatical, Viscardi discovered quickly that the site did not automatically register users the way they'd expected. Instead she had to input user information manually. Buried under the volume, by the end of the first week she was begging the CIO for help again. Volpe took the problem off her hands by having his group assume the task of registering users and answering their questions.

The project was saved through heroic efforts. But if she could do it all over again, Viscardi would opt for less heroics and more anticipation. Here's what she says she'd do differently:·

Anticipate the unwelcome outcomes of a project. "I think it would be more helpful documenting all the different scenarios that could occur and have a back-up plan in place just in case those scenarios came into reality."·

Do more homework on the vendors. "The vendors we ended up using, in hindsight, were probably not the best choice." Later, after the launch problems and before she brought the entire project back in-house, she considered using another vendor. By that time she was working closely with the CIO's group, who gave her forms to fill out that called for 12 pages of detail. "Painful as it is, it would have been nice to have done this ahead of time," Viscardi says. "I would have been more prepared. It provokes your thinking and forces you to confront things you might not have thought of."

Keeping everyone informed

You've got one more thing to plan: how to keep everyone involved up-to-date on progress against the plan, issues your team confronts, and changes that need to be made. It's not enough to agree that you'll all keep each other informed. You need a communication plan with defined deliverables and a schedule. It needs to include:

- task status reports from team members;

- project status reports for team members;

- status reports for sponsor, management, customers, and other stakeholders (including team members" managers);

- regular team meetings; and

- ways of getting and giving information, as needed, between scheduled reports and meetings.

Because these provide the basis for project control, they are covered in detail in Chapter 6. But if you don't define, schedule, and commit to them now, they won't happen – and your project may not happen either.

Are we good-to-go yet?

Let's see. You've got your purpose and objectives. You've scoped out all the required tasks into a work breakdown structure, sequenced them into a network diagram, scheduled them, and assigned your best talent to them. You've also assessed your risks and, to the extent humanly possible, made contingency plans to deal with risk events if they occur. You've committed to a communication plan that will keep everyone involved informed.

Well, bearing in mind that planning never really ends because you are constantly updating it, you should be ready to hit the ground running.

Except that we didn't want to overload this chapter, so we left out the budget. That's the next challenge.

The smartest things in this chapter

- Planning the work begins with the creation of a work breakdown structure.

- A network diagram is a map of the project with all the tasks in sequence.

- The critical path traces the longest route through the network diagram and, by doing so, reveals the shortest possible time the project will require.

- The best way to display and track a project schedule is on a Gantt Chart.

- You can track everyone's assignments on a responsibility assignment matrix.

- To avoid disastrous surprises, do a risk analysis and develop contingency plans.

Notes

1   Baker, S. and K. *The Complete Idiot's Guide® to Project Management*,
    2nd ed. Indianapolis, IN: Alpha Books, Copyright © 2000 by Sunny
    and Kim Baker.

2   Baker, S. and K. *The Complete Idiot's Guide® to Project Management*,
    2nd ed. Indianapolis, IN: Alpha Books, Copyright © 2000 by Sunny
    and Kim Baker.

5
Making Sense
out of Dollars

If budgeting your project is what frightens you most about project management, you are not alone. To new project managers, it often feels as if they are expected to pull numbers out of the air and then make them work down here on earth. Even worse, they often don't get the chance to "pull" their own numbers; senior management assigns them projects with dollar caps on them.

Since you don't have a crystal ball to predict the future, you can only calculate the best possible estimates for a project on the basis of a reasonable schedule, known resources, and management's expectations. These elements, if properly coordinated, will lead to a reasonable budget that you can use to guide your way through the project maze.

Michael C. Thomsett, *The Little Black Book of Project Management*[1]

In his book, *In Search of Excellence in Project Management*, master trainer Harold Kerzner proffers a list of common complaints from project teams. An undue proportion of them are about money, including:

- Sometimes we are pressured to cut estimates low to win a contract, but then we have to worry about how we'll accomplish the project's objectives.

- There are times when line personnel not involved in a project change the project budget.

- … equipment maintenance is a problem because there is no funding to pay for the materials and labor.

- Budgets and schedules are not coordinated. Sometimes we have spent money according to the schedule but are left with only a small percentage of the project activities complete.

- There's a lot of caving in on budgets and schedules. Trying to be a good guy all the time is a trap.[2]

If you glance over the list again, you'll notice that, while some of the complaints are directed at management, others are the result of poor budgeting within the team. So, how do you avoid that?

Is it math or magic?

For one thing, keep in mind that budgets are only as good as the cost estimates they are based upon. Unless you are Merlin the Magician, your cost estimates are only as good as the method you use to produce them.

Most project management literature talks about two ways to estimate costs: top-down and bottom-up. We'll get to those in a few paragraphs, but it's worth reckoning first with one other method, because if you had a budget handed to you at the outset of the project, there's a good chance it was done this way. It's called "rough order-of-magnitude" (ROM). James Taylor, author of *A Survival Guide for Project Managers* and *The Project Management Workshop*, says this method is based mostly on intuition and can be as much as 100 percent inaccurate.

If it's that bad, why would anyone use it? Well, we won't say people use it because their egos are so big they are convinced they are right even if they have no evidence to support their assumptions. Instead we'll look at the positive side – and there is one. Without someone having the guts to make an ROM estimate, which is really an educated guess, some projects would never get off the ground. What's management's first response to any new idea? You know the answer to that; it's a question: "What's it going to cost?"

Someone does a quick mental calculation based on vaguely similar projects done in the past (or on wishful thinking) and answers, "About $X."

That usually evokes a counter response, "Well, if we could do it for 10 percent less than that, it would be a go."

Which elicits a two-word reply, "No problem."

But of course there are problems with that kind of estimating. It's OK to do it as long as everyone recognizes that the purpose of the estimate is to start the ball rolling, to legitimize the initiation of a project. The problem occurs – too often – when people forget they pulled this number out of thin air and treat it as real and final. If you are asked to estimate the cost of a project and given no time to do more than make a quick guess, be sure you emphasize that this is just a guess and not a promise. If your numbers find their way into a written document, be even more emphatic that they must be qualified. Otherwise you might find yourself being held to them.

> Management may balk at estimates of activity costs they perceive to be high, but there is no need to be overly optimistic nor pressured to the point of underestimating just to gain a favorable reaction. Senior management will often challenge an estimate, just to see if it is defensible.
>
> Joseph W. Weiss and Robert K Wysocki, *5-Phase Project Management*[3]

How to subtract if it doesn't add up

Of course, it's one thing for you to make such an estimate, emphasizing that it is only a guesstimate, and another if senior management does it and hands it down to you as a done deal. Even if it looks as if you have no choice but to agree, to do so may be digging your own grave. If, after you've done your homework and found out how far it transcends reality, you know you can't complete the project at that cost, you would only be setting yourself up for failure if you went ahead with it. Your best approach is to document your findings on realistic costs and do some combination of the following:

- Offer an alternative: what you can do for that much money, e.g., a down-scaled version of the project that would meet the most important needs.

- Suggest other potential sources of resources that would save you enough money to come in under budget, e.g., borrow an administrative person from elsewhere in the company instead of hiring one, or use someone else's equipment during off hours. If senior management likes this idea, be sure someone agrees to put high-level clout behind obtaining those resources for you.

- Recommend extending the schedule, with additional funding in the next budget period. Show what milestones you can meet, at what cost, at what times.

Remember what you've been hearing ever since you took your first job: it's OK to bring up problems as long as you also offer a solution.

Top-down estimating

You could think of top-down estimating as what ROM should be. An educated guess still, but based upon better education: sound experience and historical data. A good top-down estimate involves talking to people who have actually led similar projects and studying previous project records. It's less a guess than an extrapolation.

You still wouldn't want to base your final budget and your cost tracking on such numbers. However, until you write your full project plan you won't have the details you need to make more precise estimates. So top-down estimates make sense for the preliminary numbers you use when you write your charter. But you should expect such an estimate to be plus/minus 25 percent, and you should note that in the charter.

Bottom-up estimating

After you've done a work breakdown structure and defined your resource requirements, you are ready to produce an estimate that is dependable using the bottom-up method. To do this, you estimate the cost of each work item, then sum them – or, in project management terminology, "roll them up" – into a total for the project. The smaller the work units, the more accurate your estimates will be.

For Northwestern Mutual's Brand Equity Project, Rick Zehner and his team used a bottom-up estimating approach.
"We took our best stab," he explains, "at what funds
were needed for key elements: redoing marketing bro-
chures, new stationery and business cards, and new signage on agencies and home office." To find out how
much each would cost, the team sought the help of experts. "We brought in the person in charge of signage to
figure out how much changing the signs would cost. We had
the person in charge of stationery come up with the best estimate with
respect to changing that. Our information systems people looked at changing electronic forms and the potential cost of that."

"We were pretty close on our estimates," he adds, "and didn't have issues
where we couldn't get funding for high priority items."

But dependable as a bottom-up estimate is, it is still only an estimate. If
you were estimating expenses on a job for an outside client, you'd certainly
build in some contingency, perhaps by creating a plus/minus range, before
you'd sign your name to the contract. Even if you are working on an internal project, give yourself some financial breathing room,
or the first time a vendor unexpectedly raises its prices,
you'll be scrambling to solve a budget crisis.

Before you start

The *PMBOK® Guide* offers a valuable list of what you
need to factor into your cost estimates, It includes such
things as:[5]

- *All work to be done.* This comes from your WBS.

- *Resource requirements for all the work.* Think broadly. Will the work entail purchases or rental of equipment and supplies, travel, professional assistance (e.g., legal), training, advertising? Will you need office or production space? And don't forget labor, even if you aren't paying for it directly – you may have interoffice charge-backs.

- *Unit rates for each resource.* This could include, for example, hourly rates for temporary workers, daily or weekly rates for rented equipment, per pound or volume measurement for bulk raw materials. Get competitive estimates from multiple vendors. And remember, almost all rates are negotiable.

- *Duration estimates.* How long will you be keeping that rented equipment, for example? The *PMBOK® Guide* also points out that if you are financing any of your resources, you also need to figure out the cost of financing.

- *Historical information* from such sources as project files, project team member knowledge, experts' knowledge.

Putting it together

Now estimating costs of each work item comes down to math – resource rates × duration – and good judgment. Do your numbers compare reasonably to historical information (allowing for inflation)? Are you making the best trade-offs among quality, availability, and price? Is there anything you've forgotten? Shuffling the numbers in various ways is a lot of work with a calculator and less so with a project management software program (and someone who knows how to use it).

When you roll these numbers up into an overall project estimate, you'll have an overall cost estimate for the project.

When you present your estimates to senior management for approval, you'll also need to include:

- Documentation of how you arrived at your numbers: resource requirements, vendor estimates, expert opinion and historical data used.

- Assumptions upon which you based your estimates, e.g., equipment price may increase over the project period due to inflation; additional people may be required during peak periods; two tasks will be able to share equipment during the period when they overlap in duration.

- A range that reasonably accommodates your contingency planning, e.g. plus/minus 10% (or more if your risks are high and the potential expenses for mitigating or coping with them are great).

From estimates to budget

Who gets how much? When? What are they expected to accomplish with it?

Those are the questions a budget is expected to answer. As the work gets done, you use it not only to dole out the money, but as one of the tools to track your performance progress. If you find, for example, that you've spent all the money you allocated for temporary help and the work you hired them for isn't done – well, that's a pretty good indication something's gone wrong. On the other hand, if the work is all done satisfactorily and you've got money left over – Hallelujah, you are in great shape.

You don't want to wait until the money is all gone to discover whether you're on track or not. That's like walking an unknown path in the dark, not knowing whether the next turn will land you in camp or in quicksand. So you will need to allocate your cost estimates not only to tasks by expense category, but also to reporting periods, perhaps monthly. That requires another close examination of your resource assignments to determine what the needs will be at any point in time. And if your money is flowing in over time, you may find you'll have to make a few schedule and resource changes to match the in-flow. That's when project management software, or at least a spreadsheet, is invaluable. You can make one change and let the software calculate its impact on the rest of the project.

Depending upon the complexity of the project, you may get away with one form that lists expense categories (equipment, supplies, labor) down the side and reporting periods along the top, with space to fill in estimates now and actual spending as the work progresses. For a bigger project, you may need forms like that for each task, or at least major milestones.

If you want to display your budget dramatically, project management professionals have a fairly simple tool for doing just that. They use a line graph that plots total projected expenditures over time. Units of time go along the top of a grid and budget money up the left side in increments from zero to the budget total. When you plot the accumulated estimates for each time period and connect them with a line, they usually form an elongated s-curve similar to the one that follows, created for a hypothetical project with total estimated expenditures of $200,000 and a total duration of six months:

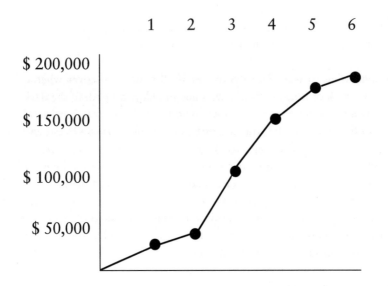

All by itself, one line on the chart may not tell you a whole lot. But once the work gets started and the money starts flowing out, you can plot actual expenditures on another line and see at a glance how well you are meeting your projections.

Back to the big question

Now let's return to the question with which we started this chapter: "How do you do a budget?"

The answer can be summed up as "You estimate your expenses, and then you allocate the total among your tasks, or deliverables, over time." Of course, that's easier said than done. And it's easier to do than to live by. But that's one of the topics in the next chapter, Making It Happen.

The smartest things in this chapter

- A top-down estimate is a ballpark guess for the whole project, based upon past experience and historical data.

- To do a bottom-up estimate, calculate the anticipated cost of each work item, then add up all the individual estimates into a total for the project.

- Senior management will want to know, not only your numbers, but also how you determined them and what assumptions you based them on.

- Be prudent. Present your estimates as ranges that accommodate your contingency planning.

Notes

1   Excerpted from *The Little Black Book of Project Management*. Copyright © 1990 by Michael C. Thomsett. Used with the permission of the publisher, AMACOM Books, a division of the American Management Association International, New York, NY. All rights reserved.

2   Excerpted from Kerzner, H. *In Search of Excellence in Project Management*. New York: Copyright © 1998 by Van Nostrand Reinhold. Reprinted by permission of John Wiley & Sons, Inc.

3   Weiss, J.W. and Wysocki, R.K. *5-Phase Project Management*. Cambridge, MA: Copyright © 1992 by Perseus Books Publishing.

4   Lewis, J.P. (1998) *Mastering Project Management*, McGraw Hill, New York. Used with permission of The McGraw Hill Companies.

5   Adapted from *A Guide to the Project Management Body of Knowledge*, 1996 ed. Newtown Square, PA: copyright © 1996 Project Management Institute.

6
Making It Happen

A project management novice purchased a recommended book on the subject. "What kind of book is this?" she scoffed, laughing. "The chapter called 'Getting Started' is more than half way through."

Well, here we are, nearly half way through this book, and it's time for you to get started – moving bricks or writing programming code or whatever has to be done to bring your project to life.

This chapter is about the delivery phase, when you execute the plan and control the work to ensure the project stays on track.

Smart quotes

Control has been described as the evil twin of planning, it is much less enjoyable, fraught with problems, and just plain hard work.

Kenneth H. Rose, "Cover to Cover," in *Project Management Journal*[1]

| | Key deliverables | | |
Conceptualization	Planning	**Delivery**	Closure
Project charter. Agreement on the purpose, intended outputs, and scope of the project. Constraints and assumptions you are operating under. Core project team. Commitment of all the stakeholders.	Project plan including project deliverables, tasks to be done, schedule, assignments, contingency plan, communication plan, and budget.	**Status reports. Project review meetings. Change requests. Updates to project plan, schedule, and budget. Milestones achieved.**	All deliverables to fulfill project goals. Final financial accounting. Full documentation of project. Final reports to customers and management. Celebration.

We've emphasized that project management was largely about planning. We even quoted someone who said if you plan well, the rest should pretty much take care of itself. Does that mean you, the project manager, can go off trekking in the Himalayas now while the project unfolds effortlessly? Well, hardly – but, of course, you knew that.

No one relaxes during the delivery phase.

Smart quotes

In the late 1970s, a large California-based defense contractor was developing a complex air defense system for the military … On the designated day for the test, all project personnel arrived at work early in the morning to ensure that the equipment was functioning correctly … The test failed … The reason was that no one had remembered to order dedicated communication lines from the phone company between the East Coast subcontractor's site and the California test site.

E.M. Bennatan, *On Time Within Budget: Software Project Management Practices and Techniques*, 3rd Edition [2]

Leading the team

So far this book hasn't focused much on the people side of project management – building and maintaining a team of committed, motivated contributors. This responsibility gets our undivided attention in subsequent chapters.

Doing project work

You'll get differences of opinion on whether or not project managers should be doing functional work at all. But, practically speaking, how much you do will depend upon the size of the project, the size of the team (if either of those is very small, you'll probably do a lot of tasks yourself), your own technical skills, and management's expectations. But there are some issues in common for all working project managers. These include:

- *Managing your time.* The larger the project, the more time you'll need to devote to managing the work, rather than doing it. Don't fall into the trap of neglecting the management side in favor of your favorite technical work – especially if it is work someone else could do.

- *Managing the impact on other project team members.* They'll appreciate it if you pitch in and work with them, proving you are not above sharing in the dirty work. But they'll resent it if they think you are hoarding the most interesting work for yourself or if they can't drag you away from your own work to help them solve a problem on theirs.

Most important, like all members of the team, *team leaders do real work themselves* ... team performance almost always depends on how well team leaders ... strike a critical balance between doing things themselves and letting other people do them.

Jon R. Katzenbach and Douglas K. Smith, *The Wisdom of Teams* [3]

Managing progress toward team goals

Usually project managers combine a formal reporting system with informal observation to keep track of the team's progress. The primary purpose of the communication plan discussed in Chapter 4 was to set you up for this. Your plan provides the structure for:

- *Obtaining task status reports from team members.* On a big project it's convenient to have a computer network that everyone can access, click on the appropriate form, and fill in the blanks. For a smaller project you can accomplish the same result with project form templates and a regular e-mail reminder to people (if necessary) to fill them out and submit them. Status report forms should include:
  - tasks completed since the last report;
  - current tasks with projected completion dates;
  - outcomes;
  - expenditures;
  - issues, potential consequences, and recommendations;
  - next steps;
  - questions; and
  - approvals needed.

Depending upon the complexity and duration of the tasks you may want these reports weekly or monthly. But if you decide on the longer reporting periods, you'll need to supplement them with frequent briefings (face-to-face if physically possible) and exception reports whenever issues arise in mid-period that could negatively impact the project scope, schedule, or budget. Exception reports need detail only issues, potential consequences, and steps taken or recommended for resolving them.

- *Preparing project status reports for team members.* You can't go wrong if you follow the advice of Andrew Gerson of AXA Client Solutions and build your report around scope, time, and cost:
  - *Scope* – completed work, approved changes, and outstanding issues, documenting who owns each issue, how it's being tracked, its priority, corrective actions planned, and when you expect it to be resolved.
  - *Time* – include a Gantt Chart showing actuals against the planned schedule.
    For example, remember the Gantt Chart for the class reunion dinner in Chapter 4. Here's what it could look like – optimistically – at the end of the second week.

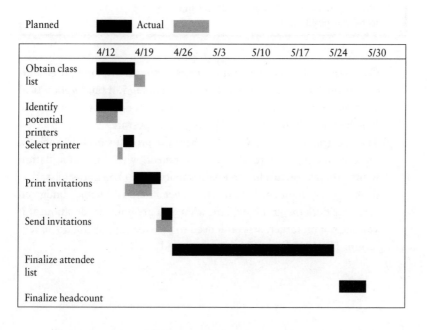

Our reunion Gantt Chart looks pretty rosy. If yours reveals a time compression that's about to explode, you'll need to address that with documentation of corrective actions taken or planned.

Golub's Laws of Computerdom

1 Fuzzy project objectives are used to avoid embarrassment of estimating the corresponding costs.

2 A carelessly planned project takes three times longer to complete than expected; a carefully planned project takes only twice as long.

3 The effort required to correct course increases geometrically with time.

4 Project teams detest weekly progress reporting because it so vividly manifests their lack of progress.

Found at: http://userpage.chemie.fu-berlin.de/diverse/murphy/murphy2.html

- *Cost* – show actuals against the budget. You can display that graphically using the line graph introduced in Chapter 5. If our hypothetical $200,000 project were running a little over budget at the end of the fourth month, it might look like the graph opposite.
  The line graph tells you visually where the project stands financially, but not how it got there. If you've overspent, why? An accumulation of little things you just haven't paid attention to? (You know what that does to your credit cards.) Or a big crucial item you hadn't budgeted for? Nor does the graph explain what you are going to do about it if you are not on target. So you'll need to provide supporting documentation. The *PMBOK® Guide* recommends including:[4]

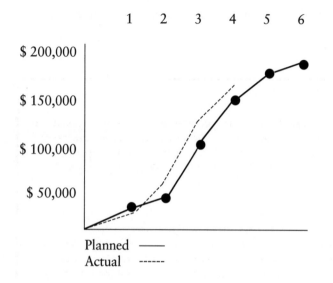

| | 1 | 2 | 3 | 4 | 5 | 6 |

$ 200,000

$ 150,000

$ 100,000

$ 50,000

Planned ——
Actual   ------

- Revised cost estimates

- Corrective action taken or planned

- Revised estimate at completion – total projected costs

- Lessons learned – why you needed the corrective action, what you or other project managers can do differently in similar situations in the future.

Never look at expenditures in isolation, without comparing them with project scope. You could get a very wrong idea even if, on your expenditures graph, everything seems to be in fine shape. In their book, *5-Phase Project Management*, Joseph W. Weiss and Robert K. Wysocki warn, "When actual expenditures are less than planned, it may be the result of being behind schedule and having not yet incurred the expenditures that were planned."[5]

AN OUNCE OF PREVENTION

The last thing you want is to burden your status reports with explanations of unnecessary budget variances. To avoid these, here's some advice from a budget veteran, Eleanor Hamill, assistant vice-president, Corporate Communications Department Administration and Special Projects, AXA Client Solutions:

- *Pay attention to minor expenses.* From paper clips to postage, the small costs can torpedo your estimates if you ignore them.
- *Keep good records.* You will need them to demonstrate how much you've done with so few resources, to answer questions about the total cost of a project, or to remind yourself of how you solved a problem when you confront it on another project.
- *Judge priorities.* Running short of money? It may be expedient to cut across the board or, on the other hand, to target tasks or deliverables with the biggest expenditures. But to meet company needs, you must consider its priorities.
- *Keep spenders informed.* If you delegate spending authority to team members, don't count on them to keep their own records. Give them regular reports or they'll be unaware of their total spending.
- *Examine bills carefully.* You'd be amazed at how often errors occur. Treat the project budget like your personal budget. If the money came out of your pocket, you'd notice mistakes like double billing or an adding error on an invoice.
- *Monitor internal charges.* Someone makes a typo on a budget code and you're incorrectly charged a few thousand dollars. It's all in the family, but it messes up your budget.

How often you need to report formally to team members varies by project. Gerson explains: "I have some projects where I have people do a flash report on certain metrics daily. Every day a 2–3 page flash report goes out to about 30 people by e-mail. In other situations a monthly report might be all that's needed."

Frequency depends upon the duration of the project, the risks involved, and the interdependency of the tasks. If you aren't sure, start off weekly. If the reports are boring, redundant, and heading straight to waste baskets (electronic or real), switch to monthly. If you can barely keep up with activity and changes in a weekly report, move to daily.

- *Preparing status reports for sponsor, management, and other stakeholders,* such as customers or others whose work your project impacts. How detailed these reports are and how frequent needs to be worked out in advance between you and the recipients. Your sponsor might want most of the details you provide to team members. It's not likely management and other interested parties will want to wade through that kind of report.

  Gerson explains the difference: "We might have a tremendous amount of control in place at the core team level, but going up, we might take a dashboard approach, just focusing on the red issues.

We really want to keep senior management informed. A regular communications memo goes out telling them what's up. If they haven't heard anything, they think nothing's being done.

Greg Winsper, AXA Client Solutions

Mike Walker, director of Capital Budgeting and Project Management at Estée Lauder, says that for projects his office oversees, the main controls at his level are against costs and against milestone dates. He asks project managers to submit monthly updates that report:

- whether or not the project is on target for "beneficial use date" – the date the project deliverable will be ready to be used by the organization; and
- issues the project team is confronting.

We provided the senior leadership team with a monthly project status report, covering overall project progress, key issues, and areas where we were falling short. Or, to put it another way:

- Where we are
- Where we need to be
- What's preventing us from getting there.

Megan Taylor, Gartner project manager

Smart quotes

In their book, *Microsoft Secrets*, Michael A. Cusumano and Richard W. Selby reveal the Bill Gates approach to project status reports. Gates told them, "I get all the status reports … [They] contain the schedule, including milestone dates, and any change in the spec, and any comments … if they want to raise an issue, that's a great way to raise it. And if they don't raise it in a status report and then two months later they say something, that's a breakdown in communication."[6]

Still, according to Gates, status reports don't have to be big, just "two screens full."[7] (It's only fitting, don't you think, that at Microsoft they measure length by screens, not pages.)

- *Facilitating meetings with the team.* Reports are indispensable for informing people, documenting actions, and maintaining historical records. But for dissecting problems, sharing points of view, and problem-solving, nothing replaces live interaction. For structuring such meetings, here's advice from Megan Taylor, who has led major corporate-wide projects for Gartner, some of them with large world-wide teams.
  - Cover deadlines, actions, issues, and accountabilities.
  - If you have team members at remote sites, have them call in.
  - Stick to an hour. Start and finish on time. Taylor sometimes had 20 people in the room all needing to speak, so she was strict about start-times.
  - Prepare and distribute the agenda in advance, assigning specific amounts of time to each topic. Let people know the deadline for submitting agenda issues.
  - If an issue is taking too much time, take it off-line for a sub-team to handle, then report back to the full team at a later meeting.
  - Bring in appropriate subject experts for each issue addressed.
  - Facilitate team problem-solving and decision-making.
  - Hold meetings on schedule, faithfully.

Taylor was describing weekly meetings. There may be times when that's not often enough, when everything is happening so fast that waiting a week to discuss an issue could doom a task to failure. If you need to switch to daily meetings – or, better yet, to supplement the weekly ones – keep them shorter and bring in only those people involved with the issues to be discussed. You can update everyone else with what Gerson calls flash reports after the meeting, if necessary, or in the weekly status reports.

- *Staying in touch informally.* You can often learn a lot more by being in the thick of the action when an issue arises than you can by reading and listening to reports afterward. One of your best tools for managing progress is just being there – dropping in on people as they work and making "how are you doing?" phone calls to team members located elsewhere. Doing this well takes tremendous people reading skills: some people thrive under the attention while others resent the surveillance. Here are some tips:

- As long as everything appears under control, don't hover. Make your visits quick. Hanging around too long wastes your time and theirs.
- Ask issue-specific questions – questions that show you really have been reading their status reports.
- Acknowledge their accomplishments.
- If they have problems, ask how you can help – and do your best to fulfill their requests. If you can't, explain why and what you can do instead.
- Offer your suggestions in terms like, "Have you tried …?" rather than "Here's what I think you should do."
- Keep your door open and make it a rewarding, not a punishing, experience to enter.

Managing changes

Did you notice how much of the section above was about managing change? If we'd left out change, we couldn't have got beyond the first progress report because change is an integral part of progressing toward the goal.

Take it as a given that there will be changes. That doesn't mean your plan was wrong or that it is useless. It's a baseline, remember, a place to move out from. It was never meant to take on the moral certainty of a tablet from Mount Sinai.

The impetus for change will come from many directions. You may confront:

- personnel changes;

- resource shortages;

- budget cuts;

- design failures;

- advances by your competitors;

- requests that you speed up delivery to meet customer requests or competitors' challenges;

- management changes that can cause your project to lose or gain favor;

- changes in organizational priorities;

- new government regulations; and

- great new ideas that you'll want to incorporate so badly you'd trade your first born for the opportunity.

Any of these can necessitate or propel changes in how you carry out your project. Thanks to your analysis of constraints and risks, you may already have contingency plans in place for some of them, allowing you to take them in stride. Others may blindside you. What you need is a change management system, an organized way to:

- identify necessary or value-added changes and avoid whimsical ones;

- keep senior management informed of worthwhile changes;

- get management approval to make changes that are outside your range of authority;

- document the changes you make and update your plan; and

- keep your sanity.

Get it in writing

Your system needs to clarify authority for making changes in project scope, schedule, and budget and define the steps in the change process. Get written clarification from your management of:

- *The range of your authority to make changes.* What kinds of spec changes can you make on your own. What expenses can you sign off on? How much contingency money do you have access to on your own authority? What changes can you make to the schedule?

- *Approvals needed to make changes outside your own authority.* Who must you go to with change requests? What information do they need to assess your requests?

- *FYIs.* Who needs to be informed of authorized changes?

Steps to take

Your company may have a standard change-management process for handling change that is outside your range of authority. Or you may need to create one with your sponsor, management, and, possibly, your customer (the person or group that is footing the bill or will benefit the most from your output). Most change management processes follow steps like these:

1   Do a team assessment of the intended change. Determine its effect on scope, schedule, and budget. Identify any negative impacts. Involve everyone on the team who would be affected by the change.

2   Document the request for change. Include the reason for the change and the projected impact of the change on scope, schedule, and budget. Don't leave out any possible negative outcomes and risks involved.

3   Deliver the request for change to everyone who needs to review it. If it's a major change, be prepared to explain and defend it in face-to-face meetings.

4   When the change is approved, update the project plan (including the schedule and budget). Don't leave an outdated, inoperative plan on the conference room wall or on your computer network while you work off some other document. That's a sure road to chaos. Redo your network diagram, Gantt chart, and any other project visuals. Post and circulate the new plan. Put the old plan away in the history file. Don't discard it. You know the law that says whatever you throw away you are going to need.

5   Circulate the revised plan to the group that approved the change.

6   Communicate the change to the entire team, clarifying how it changes their tasks and delivery dates.

7   Communicate the new plan to any stakeholders who did not have approval authority, clarifying the impact, if any, it has on them.

Documenting everything

A lot of this chapter has been about preparing documents: status reports, change requests, and plan updates. Make sure you have a central repository for all documentation, even the outdated pieces. You might even want to supplement them with a project log, sort of a Captain's Log, Stardate XXXX. In fact, some of the time you may feel as if you are lost in space. Not only does your documentation provide the answers to questions from management and stakeholders, it also has the answers when, half way through the project, the team is sitting around asking, "What did we do when … ? Haven't we tried that? What happened to … ? As a project unfolds, activity becomes history fast, but like any history, we can learn a lot from it.

Hopefully somewhere in your organization there is an accessible database of historical files from all major projects. While we stressed the uniqueness of each project early in the book, it's equally true that many aspects of projects are repeated again and again in subsequent projects. It's practically immoral to lose the lessons learned from each and start again from ground zero each time a new project is launched.

Communicating – one more time

Staying in touch with team members and other stakeholders will probably turn out to be your most time-consuming responsibility. But it's almost impossible to separate it out from the other responsibilities above. That's because it's an integral part of all of them. It includes.

- *receiving reports* from team members and discussing them;

- *reporting to upper management* and other stakeholders on progress and changes;

- *facilitating meetings* with the team to review progress, address and resolve issues;

- *facilitating ongoing interaction* among team members and between team members and other stakeholders; and

- *just maintaining contact* with all the team members, being there to help, being aware of their needs without appearing to hover or micromanage. It's a fine balancing act.

Those communications have various purposes:

- to learn;

- to inform;

- to persuade; and

- to arrive at team consensus.

To achieve these purposes, you've got a wealth of communications tools at your disposal, each of them appropriate for particular purposes:

- *reports* – to allow people to absorb information on their own time and to maintain an historical record;

- *meetings* – to get input from a group, problem-solve together, and achieve consensus, as well as to make announcements in a way that is more personal and more immediate than a memo;

- *one-on-ones* – the most personal of all, the best way to build trust;

- *video teleconferencing* – if you can afford it, the next best thing to being there;

- *conference calls* – often the only practical way to bring people in remote locations into meetings;

- *computer networks, intranets, project Web sites* – serve as both repositories for data and vehicles for exchanging information;

- *e-mail* – the fastest way to communicate the most information at the least inconvenience to everyone, but don't use it to avoid walking down the hall; and

- *fax* – rapidly being replaced by e-mail, but still an instant way to share documents across miles.

When you are the manager of a project in the Delivery Phase, you'll use every one of these media that's available to you. And if any of them aren't, start clamoring for them now.

A final word to the wise

If you are not making changes, documenting them, and communicating them during the delivery phase, then you are probably doing what Consultant Marie Scotto, of the Scotto Group, calls "playing games," and that's a sure route to disaster. What she calls "games" include:

- Fantasies such as:
  - *The estimate is a valid number.* This goes both for time and money. If you estimate a task will take 40 hours and instead it takes 60 hours, don't assume someone screwed up. Says Scotto, "The reaction should

be, 'We must have missed something. What happened?' If we keep doing this we can improve the process."

- *We don't need contingencies.* "In business," she warns, "contingency is a bad word. We call it padding. But every construction contract includes contingency."
- *We know what we're doing.* "Really," she says, "we're discovering as we go along."
- *I can do anything.* This goes along with *Whatever you want I'll give you.* What's unsaid is "But it will be crap."

- Reducing quality without telling the customer in order to deliver on time.

- Pretending the project took less time than it actually did to make yourself and the team look good.

Unfortunately, Scotto's "games" are deeply imbedded into the culture of many organizations. But they are the antithesis of good project management and they doom a project, if not to failure, then at best to mediocrity. Don't let that happen to your projects.

The smartest things in this chapter

- The Delivery Phase is when plans come to life, and your job is to manage that process.

- Status reports need to go both ways between team members and project manager. They should cover at least tasks completed, outcomes, expenditures, issues and recommendations, and next steps.

- Status reports for management and customers may focus on major milestones; changes to the scope, schedule, or costs; and issues still needing resolutions.

- Problem solving is best done face-to-face, at team meetings or one-on-ones.

- You need documentation of what changes you can authorize, whose sign-offs you need for other changes, and what processes to follow to get that approval.

- Great reports and constant e-mail can't replace regular informal contact, face-to-face as much as possible.

Notes

1   Rose, K.H. "Cover to Cover." *Project Management Journal*, June 2000.

2   Bennatan, E.M. *On Time Within Budget*, 3rd ed. New York: copyright © 2000 E.M. Bennatan. Reprinted by permission of John Wiley & Sons, Inc.

3   Katzenbach, J.R. and Smith, D.K. *The Wisdom of Teams*. Boston: Harvard Business School Press. Copyright © 1993 by McKinsey & Company.

4   Adapted from *A Guide to the Project Management Body of Knowledge*, 1996 ed. Newtown Square, PA: copyright © 1996 Project Management Institute.

5   Weiss, J.W. and Wysocki, R.K. *5-Phase Project Management*, Cambridge, MA: copyright © 1992 by Perseus Books Publishing.

6   Cusumano, M.A. and Selby, R.W. *Microsoft Secrets*, Simon & Schuster, New York. Copyright © 1995 by Michael A. Cusumano and Richard W. Selby.

7   Cusumano, M.A. and Selby, R.W. *Microsoft Secrets*, Simon & Schuster, New York. Copyright © 1995 by Michael A. Cusumano and Richard W. Selby.

Part III

The Art of Leading a Project Team

If managing a project is a science, leading a project team is an art. This part of the book covers the people side of managing projects. The art lies in molding a group of strong individuals from disparate disciplines into a unified, motivated team, committed to a common purpose and progressing toward the project goal.

Chapter 7, *Power vs. Persuasion*, focuses on the most critical skill for performing this art – the skill of effectively wielding influence – and examines how project managers, who often lack line authority, can use influence to lead the team, motivate team members, and facilitate making the decisions that move the team forward.

Chapter 8, *Is It a Team Yet?*, examines the characteristics of effective teams and the project team leader's role in guiding the team to its fullest potential.

Chapter 9, *Representing, Relating, and Advocating*, zeroes in on the relationships between the project team and people outside it, and examines the project manager's responsibilities for representing the project team to upper management, relating to outside stakeholders, and advocating for the team both inside and outside the organization.

7
Power vs. Persuasion

To get a project off the drawing board and into action, you need all the tools and techniques covered in the previous chapters. But charters don't think, network diagrams don't create, status reports don't perform. People do all that. Ultimately, managing a project comes down to managing people.

You may think of managing people in terms of running a work unit, where the manager has the authority to establish worker's priorities, assign tasks, move people from one task to another as priorities change, reward exceptional performance, and punish unacceptable performance. And employees know that, for as long as they report to you, satisfying you is their number one priority.

But managing the people on a project team isn't like that. Over the life of a project, there may be anywhere from a handful to a few hundred people working on it, depending upon its size and complexity. Chances are, hardly any of them will report to you on the organization chart. And hardly any of them will be dedicated to the project full time. They'll have other priorities to juggle, other tasks to complete, other schedules to meet, other bosses to please.

How do you convince them to put project work ahead of their other tasks and to defer to your leadership during the life of the project?

As a work unit manager you'd have line authority, but not, for the most part, as a project manager.

As a work unit manager you'd have a higher position in the hierarchy. But as a project manager, you may have team members who outrank you. And even if they don't, it doesn't mean much if they come from another part of the company and their hierarchy is different from yours.

As a work unit manager, you'd have power over your employees' performance appraisals and thus over their raises and promotions. As a project manager, you'll have, at best, a small input and possibly none at all.

As a work unit manager, you'd have reflected power since you'd represent higher management to your employees. As a project manager, you, too, have some reflected power if your project is known to be sanctioned from up above. But that power is only strong as long as upper management visibly reinforces it. It fades if the top people appear to become more interested in something else.

Smart quotes

Employees who report to multiple managers will always favor the manager who controls their purse strings. Thus, most project managers appear always to be at the mercy of the line managers.

Harold Kerzner, *Project Management: A Systems Approach to Planning, Scheduling, and Controlling,* 7th Edition[2]

> None of these people worked for me, yet they all listened to me. You have to be forceful, but not demanding, and earn respect by doing what you say you are going to do, by being willing to do whatever you ask other people to do.
>
> Megan Taylor, Gartner project manager

As a project manager, where does that leave you? Down at the bottom of every team member's priority list? Not if you learn what every successful project manager knows: that persuasion can be as effective as formal power. What you may lack in organizational authority you can make up for with personal influence.

This chapter looks at how project managers:

- acquire influence;

- use it to staff a project;

- become effective team leaders;

- keep team members motivated;

- use team members as a resource for effective decision-making; and

- increase their influence and effectiveness through skillful communication.

Smart quotes

The most difficult aspect of project management ultimately becomes the management of human resources.

William J. Brown, Hays W. "Skip" McCormick II, Scott W. Thomas, *Antipatterns in Project Management*[3]

Hans Thamhain, professor of management at Bentley College in Waltham/ Boston, Massachusetts, is a guru's guru. Author of several books and hundreds of articles on project management, he's been a major influence on other leading project management teachers and writers. Like many influential leaders in the field, he came out of an engineering background, but he is as dedicated to the people side of project work as to the quantitative side.

Earning your own authority

One challenge for project leaders, he says, is that they have to earn their own authority. "The leader has only a small degree of authority given by the organization," he explains. "The rest you have to earn yourself. You earn it by demonstrating competence and by helping people do a good job. The team doesn't need a leader to do a good report, but rather to help resolve problems, get resources, resolve conflict, and create an environment that is professionally stimulating."

Becoming a social architect

Another challenge is to build and hold together a team of part-timers. That's typical, he points out, especially in a matrix environment. The project manager, besides pulling the project together, has to have the leadership and persuasive skills to convince the functional resource managers that the project is important and to compete successfully for scarce resources.

The project team leader, he wrote in a recent article on "Leading Without Formal Authority" for the *Project Management Journal*, is a "social architect who understands the interaction of organizational and behavioral variables and can foster a climate of active participation and minimal dysfunctional conflict."

Providing a work challenge

Besides having obligations to their functional managers, team members may also be doubling up on other projects. So how do you keep team members, who have so many conflicting demands on their time, focused on your project? The most important thing you can do, according to Dr Thamhain, is to provide a work challenge. That's the strongest motivator, he stresses, for project performance. "It lowers the threshold of conflict and political intrigue," he maintains. "It increases drive and the desire to be successful. These are the requisites for commitment.

"So project managers must have both competencies in metrics – scope, timing, and resources – and people skills. Nobody can do it alone. It's all teamwork. But brilliant people are often not team players. That's where the project manager comes in, to pull it all together."

The quantitative/human link

As Dr Thamhain describes the need for both quantitative and people skills, it is clear that they aren't two separate, differentiated competencies. Rather, they are intricately linked. Here are some examples in his words:

"As the project unfolds, to maintain commitment you have to continuously provide visibility and recognition for the project. You can only do that with a decent plan. If there are no milestones, you have nothing to recognize."

"If anything, I shifted even stronger from managing by metrics to managing by people. But you cannot bring in a psychologist and think that will solve problems. You need the job skills and the administrative skills, and support systems. Without those, you lose credibility – and that brings us back to the human side."

Influence for sale here

If only you could just go out and buy it.

It's easy to spot who has influence. In a meeting a rambunctious group argues, getting louder but no closer to agreement until a quiet person in the corner speaks up and says, "I think we ought to ..." All ears perk up, all eyes turn that person's way. Everyone looks relieved and agrees, "Yes, that's right." Or, in another group, someone offers what sounds like a good idea, but there's silence until a particular person says, "Sounds good to me," and then everyone chimes in, building on the sanctioned suggestion. Or a team needs something from someone on the outside. As a group, everyone turns to one team member and implores, "You ask him. He'll listen to you."

You can see who has influence, all right, but at a glance, you may not see why. It's not always the person who has the most position power, who speaks up the fastest, loudest, or even most cleverly, or who appears to have the most friends. To acquire influence, you have to earn it. You do that by consistently demonstrating some combination of the attributes and behaviors that follow:

- *Expertise.* You've heard it many times: knowledge is power. People will look to you for leadership when you know more than they do about a key subject. Of course, as a project manager you can't possibly know more than all the team members about every technical component of the project; you've brought many of them on board precisely for their expertise. But you can and must understand the big picture better than anyone. And you must be willing to share that understanding with everyone. Ironically, you don't increase your influence by hoarding your expertise. If you do that, people will begin to wonder if it even exits or they will define you by it narrowly and shut you out of everything else.

- *Relationship building.* Take Greg Winsper's advice: "Get out of your office and tap on people's doors. Go to lunch with them. Shoot the breeze. Find out what makes them tick, what turns them on. Don't let everything be so impersonal." If you can, start the relationship building before you ever need the person's help on a project. Winsper stays alert for people who impress him, whom he might want for a future project. Also, in every business there are functions that get dumped on and get little appreciation in return. In financial services, for example, two such groups are IT and legal, Winsper says. If you think about it, you probably can pick them out in your company. You always need them, but you wish you didn't. They can speed up or slow down your project, so start building firm bridges to them now.

- *Respect for others.* Listening well is key here, especially listening without passing judgment. (There is much more about listening later in this chapter.) Accepting others' decisions shows respect too. So does welcoming feedback from others on your behavior.

- *Quid pro quo.* Spread a few favors around. People remember and they'll be there to help when you need them. Of course there's a fine line between the beloved person that others would face a firing squad for and the one whose good deeds elicit a suspicious, "Wonder what she wants in return."

- *Trustworthiness.* Without trust, influence doesn't exist. Some perverted form of it might – fear, intimidation, coercion – but not influence in any positive sense. People are comfortable allowing themselves to be influenced by someone they trust to tell the truth (both good and bad), give credit where it is due, accept accountability when things go wrong, and care more about the outcome of the project than about personal aggrandizement. How do you earn that kind of trust? In their book, *The New Why Teams Don't Work*, Harvey Robbins and Michael Finley, offer these strategies:[4]

1 Have clear, consistent goals.
2 Be open, fair, and willing to listen.
3 Be decisive.
4 Support all other team members.
5 Take responsibility for team actions.
6 Give credit to team members.
7 Be sensitive to the needs of team members.
8 Respect the opinions of others.
9 Empower team members to act.

Most importantly, trust is a two-way street. You have to extend it to earn it. You have to trust team members to do things that may be beyond your comfort level, such as representing the project to customers, assigning responsibilities, and making decisions about things that affect them. And if they screw up, you've got to trust them to learn from it, and help them to do so.

SMART VOICES

> Bill Crockett's Trust-Building Techniques
>
> - Walk the talk.
> - Listen to team members, and really follow up.
> - Show evidence that you are helping.
> - Recognize when the team's performance is good; tell members when performance is not good, but ...
> - Don't beat them up for failure in a learning situation; instead show them where they might do better next time.
> - Be the team's advocate.
>
> From *The Team Coach* by Donna Deeprose[5]

As a project manager, your ability to get your needs met through influence gets tested before the project team goes to work. You need it first to entice people onto the team and get their work unit managers to support their participation.

Staffing up

Greg Winsper's strategy sessions, described in Chapter 2, illustrate a potent use of influence to build a project team. Early in the conceptualizing stage, he pulls together a group of managers whose help he'll need for a day of brainstorming about the project. By lunch, they're asking where they can sign up. By the end of the day, they realize they have already put their mark on the project and are beginning to feel a sense of ownership. They go back to their offices eager to commit their own time or that of their employees to the project.

It's passion for the project that binds the team members and their managers to it, Winsper maintains.

> Q. "What's in it for me?"
> A. Prepare yourself to answer that question every time you ask a line manager to contribute an employee to your project team. Be ready to tell the manager how the outcome of the project will benefit that work unit and what the employee will learn on the project team that can be applied back at home base.

Smart answers to tough questions

Irwin M. Jacobs is a division manager at Science Applications International Corporation (SAIC) in McLean, VA. SAIC is the largest employee-owned research and engineering company in the United States. As well as heading up a division, he often manages projects for clients, which may require some skills his division does not possess. He seeks out the talent he needs from elsewhere in the company and then negotiates with the individuals and their managers to bring them on board. On a recent project for the Marine Corps, only three of eight team members, including himself, resided in his division. "The people have to be willing to operate as part of your team," he says. Convincing them and keeping them requires influencing skills.

"Typically, what an individual will say is, 'I'm about 75 percent covered now, but let me talk to my boss and see if I can give you 25 percent,'" Jacobs explains. Or, if he's done a still better influencing job, the same person might say, "I really like your project. Let me see if my manager will relieve me of 25 percent of my other work, so I can give you 50 percent of my time."

How does he formalize the arrangement? "Probably a handshake with the other divisional manager seals it," he says.

Admittedly, influence goes only so far. You may not always get the people you choose for your project team. They may be totally locked in to other tasks or their managers may resist your strongest persuasion. You may have to compromise and accept someone else, someone whose skills or team commitment is unknown or, worse, inferior. Your team may be pre-selected for you, without your input. Or you may get a person you want, but only because your sponsor or some other high-ranking individual put some authoritarian muscle behind your request. That can work and you may have to fall back on it sometimes, but it can also cause resentment in both your team member and her work unit manager. In any of these situations, your influencing skills are even more essential as you take on the challenge of leading this team to project success.

What team leaders do – and how they do it

"Managing is controlling, taking charge of, directing, administering," Jacobs asserts. "Leading is influencing people. You do that by persuasion. You have to lead the people on your team to get the job done."

To become an effective team leader, a good place to start is with six guidelines offered by Jon R. Katzenbach and Douglas K. Smith, in their book, *The Wisdom of Teams.*[6]

1 Keep the purpose, goals, and approach relevant and meaningful.

2 Build commitment and confidence.

3 Strengthen the mix and level of skills.

4 Manage relationships with outsiders, including removing obstacles.

5 Create opportunities for others.

6 Do real work.

Meaning and relevance

Especially when projects are destined to take a year or two, it's easy for teams to lose sight of their final goal. Sometimes teams confuse the accomplishment of a single milestone with project success. It's not likely that a construction crew would walk away after completing the first floor of a skyscraper. But in a team formed to coordinate the output in a newly merged conglomerate, one member recalls how the team ran out of steam after its first accomplishment, the publication of a joint catalog for one market.

And in another team, a subgroup preparing one component got so bogged down in its pursuit of perfection in all details that it lost track of its main purpose, to integrate its component with several others into a final product.

"Teams expect their leaders to … help the teams clarify and commit to their mission, goals, and approach," stress Katzenbach and Smith.[7] You can do that by scheduling time into project review meetings to review the purpose and goals. Have the team ask itself:

• Has anything changed in the economy, technology, society, or our company that impacts our purpose and goals?

• Is our purpose still relevant?

• Is our final goal still appropriate?

• Is our approach still the best way to achieve that goal?

• If not, what modifications should we make?

• What's our next step?

You don't need to do this every week, but it's a good idea to do it upon the completion of each milestone and certainly if you see commitment lagging in the team or you foresee an external change that could throw the team into turmoil. And remember Marie Scotto's advice about meeting in front of a large, posted network diagram. It's a great graphic reminder of where the team is supposed to be going.

Commitment and confidence

Katzenbach and Smith emphasize that this applies to individuals as well as to the team as a whole. What they are talking about here is using positive feedback rather than intimidation to keep the team in action. You can boost commitment and confidence among your team members by meeting with them individually to acknowledge the work they've done, placing special emphasis on how that work contributes to the team goal. "Joe, thanks for the great job you did on the market research," isn't good enough. You need to get specific and let Joe know that, "Thanks to your data on the importance of the over-55 segment, we're going to totally revise our target markets. We'll leave the competition in the dust."

Skills – both technical and interpersonal

In the best of all possible worlds, you'd start your project with a team of the best technical and business minds in your organization, all of them, incidentally, proven to be great team players. Those people would stick with the project from beginning to end, augmented when necessary by other top-notch specialists in functions you need only for a brief time.

It could happen to you, but don't count on it.

Here are the kinds of things that determine the makeup of real-life teams. You ask a functional manager to lend you a person with a particular expertise, and the manager sends you a novice for whom your team will be a great training opportunity. There's a particular skill you need, and the only person who has it is a loner who grudgingly agrees to work for the team, but sits alone at every meeting, saying nothing unless directly asked. And just when you think you finally have the all bases covered, a team member with a unique skill leaves the company – and leaves you stranded.

Nevertheless there are things you can do to build and maintain a team with a wide range of strong skills:

- Pair a less experienced team member with a more experienced one on tasks. This gives the novice an opportunity to observe and learn and gives the more experienced one the chance to develop a replacement on some tasks or at least someone who can eventually lighten the load.

- Pair up business and technical people so they learn from each other. After working with technical people for the life of an important Gartner project, an auditor learned enough to move into a technology department when the project was over.

- Create sub-teams where a loner works closely with one or two other people in situations where their work is interdependent and they have to communicate with each other to complete their tasks. Use outside consultants for only as long as it takes for a team member to become proficient at the role the consultant plays.

- Have bench strength. Don't settle for one person possessing a cluster of unique and necessary skills. If you don't have at least two people on your team capable of doing every task, then make sure you know where you can acquire someone in a hurry.

Relationships with outsiders

As well as reporting to upper management and updating customers and other stakeholders, it's your job to stand up to critics and fight for the team's right to scarce resources. The more the team observes you going to bat for the project and the people working on it, the more credibility you build as a leader. In fact, this is such an important part of the project team leader's role that Chapter 9 is devoted to it.

Opportunities for others

You can create learning and growth opportunities for team members by:

- Assigning them to high-profile tasks, especially those that require interaction with upper management. Let's say your project is to develop a new information retrieval system for all departments. Meeting with a department head to do a needs analysis and incorporating that department's needs into the system is an opportunity for a team member to contribute something important and gain visibility.

- Asking them about specific interests or long-term personal goals and giving them assignments that are stepping stones toward their own goals. Someone with writing aspirations would be the perfect person to produce a project newsletter.

- Providing training, either on-the-job along with an experienced person or at outside seminars or courses.

- Rotating the role of meeting facilitator. You get a break and they get experience.

- Sharing the spotlight by taking a team member along to meetings with upper management.

- Creating sub-teams, each with its own team leader, to take on large tasks.

- Rotating team member responsibilities. It gets everyone's juices flowing to take on different tasks.

"Real" work

You've got to get your hands dirty along with the rest of the team. While it may be necessary for you to take a piece of the project as your own and do the technical work on it, that isn't what this means. In fact, when you do that you have to be very careful not to appear to be keeping the most interesting work for yourself. And you can't let your technical work take priority over supporting the other team members or tracking project progress. These things can backfire and set you up as a scapegoat if anything goes wrong.

What does win you respect and loyalty is pitching in when the going gets rough: when there's all night collating to do, a rushed proofreading and editing job, or last minute code to write (if you can write code – if you can't, bring coffee and cookies); when everyone works all weekend to box and mail your test product to hundreds of recipients; or the administrative assistant gets sick and someone has to handle the phones.

It's ironic but it's human nature. They'll hold you in awe for doing the most mundane things. And they'll want to work for you – or, more aptly, with you. But they'll resent you for playing a starring technical role.

And a warning from the experts

Along with their six things for team leaders to do, Katzenbach and Smith also stress two things never to do: "they do not place blame or allow specific individuals to fail and they never excuse away shortfalls in team performance."

Mistakes and shortfalls aren't failure. They are opportunities to learn.

But some days you'd rather just stay in bed

Wouldn't we all, including your project team members! And sometimes they give in to it, mentally if not physically. Motivation lags. Team members start to miss meetings or, worse yet, deadlines. Project work falls to the bottom of their priorities list. Even someone who has been attacking project tasks with energy and enthusiasm may go into a funk.

When these things happen, the team needs (a) jumpstarting and (b) ongoing motivational fixes.

When the whole team drags, the project team leader often can jump start it by a combination of celebrating its successes to date, demonstrating appreciation for team members' efforts so far, and refocusing on the project goal. That could mean spontaneously turning a project review meeting into a champagne party with gag awards for everyone tied to memorable events, followed up – now that everyone is mellow and feeling pretty positive – with a serious re-examination of the project purpose, goals, and approach (as described earlier in this chapter).

That should work for about a week. But that's long enough to start figuring out how you can help team members retain their energy and enthusiasm for the length of the project.

> You have to instill the passion in people – that they really, really want to see this come into being. With passion, they'll wake up in the morning and this is the thing they'll want to work on.
>
> Greg Winsper, AXA Client Solutions

SMART VOICES

There's plenty of literature on motivating workers. And, to get them out of the way now, there are purists who say motivation is internal and you can't "give" it or "do" it to anyone else. But that's just semantics, and anyway *Webster's Dictionary* has no problem with the idea of motivating someone else so that's good enough for us.

Let's be clear. This book is going to use the word "motivate" to mean:

To inspire people to do work to the best of their ability by creating an environment in which they get satisfaction from doing the work itself.

Even the purists can't object too strongly to that definition.

Motivating team members, by that definition, is one of the key responsibilities of project team leaders. The next question, of course, is: *how?*

What motivates workers?

Some recent surveys provide answers you can use. Dr Kenneth Kovach of George Mason University in Fairfax, Virginia, asked 1000 employees to rank order 10 job rewards in terms of motivational value. Topping the respondents' lists were:

1   Interesting work; and

2   Full appreciation of work done.

He also asked their supervisors what they thought their employees wanted. Boy did they have it wrong! Supervisors said 1) good wages and 2) job security. In fact, workers and supervisors have been responding to this identical survey periodically since 1946 and supervisors have gotten it wrong every time. So, just in case you tend to think like these supervisors, you're going to need to shake up your mindset a little. But it should be a welcome change. As a project manager, you can probably do a lot more to provide interesting work and appreciation than you can to raise your team members' wages or offer job security.

Another study came up with slightly different, but complementary information. According to the Families and Work Institute of New York, the most powerful predictors of productivity are:

• higher job quality – autonomy, learning opportunities, meaning, and a chance to get ahead; and

• supportive workplaces – helping workers become more effective workers, people, and parents.

You've got the power

You may not have line authority, but you do have the power to provide the four things the studies say are the best motivators.

Interesting work

By its very nature, project work is interesting – at least to the person or people who thought up the project. It's aimed at accomplishing something new; it's unpredictable because it hasn't been done before; it offers opportunities to work with people in other departments and other functions. It's definitely not the "same old, same old."

But no project comes without its share of drudgery. For every breakthrough outcome, the project may require hundreds of phone calls, pages of letters and reports, hours spent in meetings rehashing the same issues, weeks of testing components, more weeks or months of meticulous rework. After a while, even to the most passionate project supporters this kind of work is about as interesting as another Brady Bunch rerun.

Still, nobody demands that work be interesting all the time. Your job is to ensure that everybody gets a share of the good part. Here are some ways to do that:

- *Divide the creative work into small enough tasks so that everyone gets a piece*, but a big enough piece to inspire a sense of ownership. "The need to have a piece of ownership that they can put a mark on," underscores Greg Winsper.

- *Avoid depending too much on a few superstars*, while asking the regular folk to do all the back-up work. You may think you are ensuring project success that way, but you are risking burning them out while turning off your other team members. In the long run, your project will benefit from developing a wider group of contributors. And you may uncover a star in the making.

- *Empower team members* to determine for themselves how they will do their tasks – and to continually look for better ways to do things.

- *Ask people what tasks outside their own specialties they would like to assist on*. It's a great way to them learn something new.

- *Pair up people from different specialties* to work together on tasks that combine both sets of skills.

- *Pair novices with experts.* The less experienced people learn, you build bench strength, and the more experienced people eventually get to turn over some of their workload.

- *Rotate people among the project's tasks.* If your project lasts more than a couple of months, don't lock anyone into doing the same thing the whole time. When people switch jobs, it gives them a fresh start and brings a new perspective to each task that can move the project along.

- *Share the drudgery, too.* Instead of assigning one person to spend a week making phone calls, for example, bring in five people (including the prima donnas and yourself) to spend one day. Misery does love company.

- *Add fun to the humdrum.* Still using our phone call marathon as an example, give prizes for the most calls, most unsuccessful attempts to reach the same person, weirdest excuse for not answering – whatever inspires pride or laughter. Take periodic breaks to play. Cubicle walls make fine volleyball nets.

- *Relate the routine to the final outcome.* This adds meaning to the task and makes it more palatable. Approaching one more phone call thinking, "This is number 38 out of 100," is pretty discouraging. It helps to think, "I'm getting one more piece of information that will help determine the market for our new product."

Appreciation

There are plenty of ways to show your appreciation for a team member's contributions. Here's a sampling:

You're going to need those people for your next project and you won't get their passion if you don't recognize them. It can be as simple as dropping a handwritten note in the mail – not e-mail – to their boss, cc-ing the appropriate parties. Hopefully the boss will write a note on it and send it down.

Greg Winsper, AXA Client Solutions

- *Send a letter to the team member,* copying the person's work unit manager, referring specifically to the task done and emphasizing its contribution to the project outcome.

- *Write to the team member's work unit manager,* copying the team member, describing the importance of the member's contributions to the project.

- *Acknowledge the individual's work in your status report* to upper management. Give credit where it's due. Make sure the individual gets a copy.

- *Acknowledge the work of a team member or sub-team at a project review meeting.* But be sensitive to the reaction of the individual. Some people find this embarrassing.

- *Give team members added visibility.* When you meet face-to-face with your sponsor or a management review team, take a member along.

- *Make it tangible.* Give out awards, not expensive ones; this really is a case of it's being the thought that counts. Teams have used caps, paperweights, mugs, even bugs as symbols of appreciation. Find knick-knacks that symbolizes your team or order some paperweights engraved with your team logo. The items you choose can be serious or humorous – a sense of humor goes a long way when you are working with other people. Give the awards out to team members to acknowledge their accomplish-

Once [Sherri Lindenberg of AXA] gave all members of a team she led 10-minute phone cards that an outside vendor had left with her. "The card itself didn't mean that much, but it called attention to their participation and showed I valued it."

Donna Deeprose, *Recharge Your Team*[8]

ments. We all say we don't want any more tchatchkas, but we like other people to know we got them.

- *Put a feature into the company (or the team's own) newsletter or intranet*, focused on the work of a sub-team. Every accomplishment deserves to be singled out this way.

- *Celebrate the team's accomplishments*. Mark each milestone with a party. Have cake and coffee or wine and cheese brought in just to tell people you appreciate how hard they are working on a particularly tough task.

- *Say "Thank you,"* the simplest of all – two words spoken sincerely. You don't need line authority to show appreciation. What you do need, to make it meaningful, is to follow some important guidelines:

- *Do it often* enough to be noticed, but not so often that it becomes white noise.

- *Be very specific* about what earned your appreciation, and about its contribution to the project. "Thanks for proofreading," sounds pretty mechanical. "Thanks to you, we'll make our deadline for delivering the report to the customer, and we won't have egg on our face because we spelled his name wrong," has a lot more impact.

- *Be sincere.* Appreciation is not a management technique, it's a sentiment. People who toss kudos around like tennis balls get pegged as phonies very fast. The closer you stay in touch with the work people are doing, the more you'll find to be sincerely appreciative about.

Higher job quality

At the very least, each team member's contribution to the project makes a fine résumé addition. So be sure to put each team member's contributions in writing for her when she leaves the project. Project work should also increase her skills, her network of contacts within the organization, and her visibility to upper management and other parts of the company. Many project team members find ways to apply what they learned on the project to their full-time jobs, making those broader and more interesting. You can help her make all these things happen.

Supportive workplaces

Remember that people do have lives outside their jobs. Try not to make 24/7 a status symbol on your team. And be understanding when people want to schedule their project work around personal events.

Team decision making – a great motivator (and good business)

The very best way to keep team members energized by your project is to empower them to make the decisions that determine what they will do and how they'll do it. They'll have a lot more loyalty to their own decisions than to yours.

If that's scary – after all, you are the one who is ultimately accountable – keep reminding yourself that you brought them on to the project for their skills and their smarts. So take advantage of them. In most cases the best decisions are made by team consensus.

The biggest drawback to consensus decision-making is time. You probably don't have time to waste, so let's acknowledge here that there are situations when consensus is not the best approach. Let's get those exceptions out of the way now. You don't need a team to make a decision when:

- *The building is burning.* An emergency may force you to make a decision right away. (For that matter, an emergency may force one of your team members to make a decision right away, too, and in those circumstances you will need to support it.)

- *Only one person has the expertise required* to make the decision. The last thing you want is to have a bunch of non-techies arguing about what programming language to use. But don't confuse expertise with knowledge. Don't make a unilateral decision because only you know something upper management plans to do. You can share knowledge.

- *Only one person or a sub-group will be affected* by the decision. Bringing the whole team together to decide what graphics software your artists should use is a waste of time.

- *The team can't reach consensus.* If despite everyone's best efforts, team members simply can't agree on the right path to take, the team needs an arbitrator – probably you or the sponsor. It's a good idea for the team to agree in advance on how much time they will devote to consensus building and that, if arbitration is necessary, they'll all support the decision.

"You'd like stakeholders to all agree," concurs Karen Cone, senior vice-president at Gartner, whose World Class Web project involved hundreds of people during the same time Warren and Viscardi were building the alumni Web site. "But if they can't it's going to get escalated. When a dispute is arbitrated, a real team will say, "OK, we're going to implement against that even if we don't like it."

Steps to consensus

Exceptions aside, decisions that affect the whole team are best made by the whole team. That requires skill at consensus building. If you don't have that experience, you might want to bring in a professional facilitator. If you choose to facilitate, here are guidelines to follow for problem solving/ decision-making by consensus:

1 *Identify the real need.* Sometimes what looks a problem that needs to be solved is only a symptom. Get to the heart of the issue before you start making decisions. You'll have to question, prod, and listen. The team may need to do some additional research.

2 *Encourage everyone to participate.* Silence is not assent; it's dissent, warns one team champion. Don't count on a person who says nothing to participate in implementing the decision once it's made.

3 *Collect and analyze data.* Discussing an issue usually reveals gaps in everyone's knowledge. The team can't make an informed decision until those gaps are filled. Coming to a shared understanding of the data makes joint decision-making easier.

My role is to facilitate: Give equal floor space to everyone and resolve issues quickly. Make sure the appropriate people are brought in to address issues and problems. Don't shut people out, give people respect, build on what people say, and interrupt nicely if someone goes on too long. Ensure that information flows freely and everyone is getting a benefit. It's not easy, especially with headstrong, intelligent people trying to get their points across. Sometimes it turns into debates.

Megan Taylor, Gartner project manager

4   *Determine the criteria their decision must meet.* What must happen and what must not happen? This often means balancing three needs: time, cost, and product requirements.

5   *Brainstorm solutions.* Keep it freewheeling. Invite people to elaborate on others' ideas. Encourage quiet team members to participate. Ask them what they'd do if there were no restrictions. Sometimes one person's outrageous ideas inspires someone else's very targeted one. Don't discount any ideas yet because they don't seem to meet the criteria. That's the next step, after ideas are exhausted.

6   *Weigh potential decisions against the criteria.* One way is to make a matrix with criteria across the top and the alternatives down the side. Team members rate each alternative against each criterion on a scale of 1–5, then total the scores. This doesn't mean the one with the highest score is the answer, but it's a way to eliminate impossible ones and highlight the best few. Sometimes in the process, new variations on the alternatives get generated.

7   *Commit to the decision.* Focus on where people agree. You may be able to combine parts of two or more alternatives into one consensus decision. Get a verbal commitment from everyone to support one decision.

8   *Develop an implementation plan,* including steps to take, a schedule to follow, and specific tasks for individuals and sub-teams.

Remember, consensus doesn't mean everyone loves it; it means they can all support it.

> Consensus-building tools
>
> - Straw votes – to limit the options to a manageable number
> - Making modifications – to win over a holdout
> - Creating combinations – when two or three choices are better than one
> - Airing reservations – to avoid groupthink or passive resistance
> - Reassessing and re-evaluating – to get a fresh start
> - Taking a break – when progress bogs down
> - Having trial runs – to lessen the fear of making a mistake
>
> Donna Deeprose, *The Team Coach*[9]

Communication – the key skill

If a genie ever offers you just one request and you want to use it to leverage your influence and improve your leadership, ask to become a better communicator. Not a better speaker, but a better communicator – there's a difference and it's an important one.

Communicating skillfully and genuinely is the mark of a successful leader. It's part technique and part integrity. You can learn the techniques. Here are the most important ones:

- *Do it face-to-face whenever possible.* Body language, eye contact, facial expressions, voice tone – all these tell at least as much, if not more, than words. You lose them all in e-mail and most of them on the phone.

- *Listen more than you talk.* We learn so much more that way and even express ourselves better through our listening. Think about the last time you had a real heart to heart with someone: What made a bigger impression, her words or when she really paid attention to you? The keys to good listening include:

  1 *Pay attention.* Stop thinking about your own next statement and really hear the speaker out. Demonstrate your attentiveness by leaning slightly forward. (You don't have to be rigid about it. You can relax back, and then come forward again at important points.) Acknowledge audibly with an occasional "uh huh" or "hmm." There's a place for polite grunts. Do not tap a pencil or shuffle papers.

  2 *Ask just enough questions to encourage the speaker* to support his statements with more details. Don't ask so many that you challenge him or shift the direction of the topic.

  3 *Confirm your understanding* periodically by paraphrasing what the speaker has said. You can start with a phrase like, "If I understand you correctly, you're suggesting ..." It's amazing how often people walk away from a conversation with totally different ideas of what was said. You can ensure that doesn't happen.

  4 *When the speaker has finished, sum up* what he said in a few sentences: "Let me confirm this, your main concerns are ..."

  5 *It's your turn*; you've earned it. Look for points of agreement to start your response. Build on those as much as possible, then state your concerns with the intention of finding common ground.

Yes, it's much more work to listen than to lead the conversation. That's why people talk more than they listen.

- *Use your role as a project manager to move information 360 degrees.* Keep the team informed of management's moves that affect the project. Keep management well informed of the team's progress and its issues (before they become unassailable hurdles). Do the same with other stakeholders inside and outside the organization.

- *Provide opportunities for team members to share information* with each other. Encourage them to get together outside the formal project review meetings where the agenda is tight and people are anxious to escape.

It takes more than skill

That's the technique side of communicating. The other side is integrity. That requires:

- *Telling the whole truth.* Share with the team everything you know that could affect the project. Don't hide bad news for fear of driving people away. They'll only resent you for it when they find out.

- *Sharing the glory.* In all your communications outside the team, emphasize that this is a team project and the successes belong to the team.

- *Not blaming.* Screw-ups happen. Examine them to find out why so they don't recur, but not to find a scapegoat.

Come to think of it, technique and integrity probably sum up not just what's required to communicate well, but the underpinnings of the project manager's whole job.

The smartest things in this chapter

- Project managers lead through influence, not authority.

- Your influence grows as you demonstrate expertise, show respect for others, do people favors, and prove yourself trustworthy.

- Studies have shown that what motivates people most are interesting work, appreciation, improvements in job quality, and supportive workplaces.

- You get better decisions and greater commitment when teams make decisions by consensus.

- To increase your influence, work on your communication skills, especially listening.

Notes

1   Barr, L. and N. *The Leadership Equation.* Austin, TX: Eakin. Copyright © 1989 by Lee and Norma Barr.

2   Kerzner, H. *Project Management: A Systems Approach to Planning, Scheduling, and Controlling,* 7th ed. New York: Copyright © 2000 Harold Kerzner. Reprinted by permission of John Wiley & Sons, Inc.

3   Brown, W.J., McCormick, H.W. III, and Thomas, S.W. *Antipatterns in Project Management.* New York: Copyright © 2000 by William J. Brown, Hays W. "Skip" McCormick, and Scott W. Thomas. Reprinted by permission of John Wiley & Sons, Inc.

4　From *The New Why Teams Don't Work*, 2nd ed. copyright © by Harold Robbins and Michael Finley. Reprinted with permission of the publisher, Berrett-Koehler Publishers, Inc., San Francisco CA. All rights reserved.

5　Excerpted from *The Team Coach*. Copyright © 1995 by Donna Deeprose. Used with the permission of the publisher, AMACOM Books, a division of the American Management Association International, New York, NY. All rights reserved.

6　Katzenbach, J.R. and Smith, D.K. *The Wisdom of Teams*. Boston: Harvard Business School Press. Copyright © 1993 by McKinsey & Company.

7　Katzenbach, J.R. and Smith, D.K. *The Wisdom of Teams*. Boston: Harvard Business School Press. Copyright © 1993 by McKinsey & Company.

8　Excerpted from *Recharge Your Team*, by Donna Deeprose. Copyright © 1998 American Management Association. Used with the permission of the publisher, American Management Association International, New York, NY. All rights reserved.

9　Excerpted from *The Team Coach*. Copyright © 1995 by Donna Deeprose. Used with the permission of the publisher, AMACOM Books, a division of the American Management Association International, New York, NY. All rights reserved.

8

Is It a Team Yet?

Historically, project management was viewed as a scheduling tool to be used by engineers. But project management is more than planning and scheduling. It's working with teams, motivating them, and getting them to accomplish an objective. In fact, the behavioral side is more important than the quantitative techniques.

Harold Kerzner, professor of systems management at Baldwin-Wallace College and executive director, International Institute of Learning

SMART VOICES

"Team" has been a hot word for several years now. It's been applied to everything from a small, self-managed permanent work group to an entire 50,000-person conglomerate. But nowhere is it more appropriate than when it's used for a group of people brought from various functions to work together on a project. All the characteristics that define a true team are the very attributes necessary to make a project successful.

A *true* team? What exactly is that? Jon R. Katzenbach and Douglas K. Smith defined it best in their book, *The Wisdom of Teams*:

> *A team is a small number of people with complementary skills who are committed to a common purpose, performance goals, and approach for which they hold themselves mutually accountable.*[1]

SMART PEOPLE
TO HAVE ON
YOUR SIDE:

JON R.
KATZENBACH

Jon R. Katzenbach has probably had more influence on the way people think about teams in business than anyone else. For many people, *The Wisdom of Teams*, the book he co-authored with Douglas K. Smith, is the ultimate authority on the potential of teams and what's needed to achieve that potential.

When the book came out in the early 1990s, many people still shrugged off teams as a fad and asked, "Why bother?" The book's responses to that question are as powerful today as they were then:

- "First, [teams] bring together complementary skills and experiences that, by definition, exceed those of any individual on the team."
- "Second, in jointly developing clear goals and approaches, teams establish communications that support real-time problem-solving and initiative."
- "Third, teams provide a unique social dimension that enhances the economic and administrative aspects of work … people on teams build trust and confidence in each other's capabilities."
- "Finally, teams have more fun … it both sustains and is sustained by team performance."[2]

Katzenbach's other books include *Real Change Leaders*, *Teams at the Top*, and *Peak Performance*. In addition, he is editor of *The Work of Teams*. He is a founder of Katzenbach Partners LLC and was formerly a director of McKinsey & Company, Inc.

It's a team when ...

- *Members have a common purpose and they need each other to attain it.* This is why working on a project is so different from working in most permanent work units, where people may call themselves a team but in fact they are usually working individually, in parallel.

Ask a marketing professional what work he does and he'll probably tell you he's in charge of marketing products x, y, and z. To do his job, as he defines it, he doesn't need his colleague who markets products a, b, and c, except for someone to have lunch with and bounce ideas off occasionally.

But ask him about the cross-functional project team he's on, and he'll say, "I'm on a team to develop and market products that will make us the industry leader in the over-50 market." He defines his role in terms of the team purpose, and he knows he can't achieve it alone.

Lest this smugly sounds as if participating in a project automatically bestows successful team status, it's not that easy. In fact, novice project managers often assign discrete tasks to individuals with appropriate skills and send them off to work independently of each other. In effect, what they create is not a team at all but a group of individuals working in parallel tracks, just like those typical of many work units.

But what works in a line organization doesn't work in a project where everything must coordinate. The result can be a disaster like the tale of the two sub-teams building components for a large vehicle. Working in isolation from each other, the sub-teams lost sight of their purpose – to build a new vehicle – and focused totally on building their

SMART VOICES

We are usually much better at dividing up the work than at drawing people together under a common banner.

Geoffrey M. Bellman,
*Getting Things Done
When You Are Not in Charge*[3]

separate components. One sub-team got a great idea for improving its component. The only problem was that the "improvement" changed the piece just enough so that when they were finished the two components didn't fit together.

If you are thinking that story demonstrates a catastrophic lack of control, you're right. But unless you personally are an expert in all the technical aspects of your projects and can clone yourself and be everywhere at once, don't try to assume that control alone. True teams handle that control collectively.

• *Team members agree on goals to achieve the purpose, tasks to meet the goals, and standards for success.* This is a tough lesson for new project managers who are not used to working with teams. Mike Walker, director of Capital Budgeting and Project Management at Estée Lauder, says it's crucial for project managers to learn to work this way. "We teach them, 'Define the need; don't tell me the solution. Let the project team, afterward, recommend the solution.'"

Because team members set the goals and create the plan, they are accountable for living up to their own expectations. They are also responsible for revisiting, revising, and improving the goals and plan as they go along.

• *Members hold themselves individually and collectively accountable for team results.* When you see evidence of this, you know you've got a real team. It doesn't happen automatically just because people are assigned to the project. In fact, at first people will probably define their responsibilities narrowly: this is my task; that is your task. If a deadline slips, they'll look for a person to blame.

A project leader would … get the main project team together and have them create a work breakdown structure … Then she'd lead the team through the process of creating a deliverables schedule that would show each subproject interim and final deliverable. These dates would be set by the members of the team, based on their own schedules and the needs of the project. The subproject leaders would then go off and lead their subproject teams through a similar participative process to schedules of deliverables.

Paula K. Martin and Karen Tate, "More Power to the Team," *PM Network*[4]

But as the project begins to take shape, their investment in it grows until, rather than pointing fingers when a problem occurs, their first reaction will be: "How can we fix this? How can we be sure it doesn't happen again?" That's when team members volunteer to help each other get over a hump, offer to share resources with each other, and come up with creative ways to adjust their own schedules to lessen the impact of the missed deadline.

As a project manager, there are things you can do to accelerate your team's development to this level of accountability:

- Set an example by not placing blame. Treat mistakes and missed deadlines as an opportunity to improve the process.
- Keep the team focused on the purpose and goals, revisiting them regularly.
- Reward members who go the extra mile to achieve team goals.
- Celebrate the achievement of project milestones.
- Encourage team members from different line organizations to work together on tasks.

More characteristics of successful teams

Katzenbach and Smith relate team success to some additional characteristics:

- *Size*. It should be small enough, they maintain, that you can communicate easily with everyone. Each member should be familiar with the role and skills of all other members.

  If your project requires a cast of hundreds, don't despair. Keep the core team small and make them leaders of sub-teams. You'll still need to keep your finger on the pulse of all the activity, but you can do that primarily through your core team. Try to get to know all the players, but you needn't meet with them all weekly.

- *Complementary skills*. Katzenbach and Smith define three kinds of skills: technical, problem-solving/decision-making, and interpersonal. You probably won't find equal measures of all three skills in all your team members, but choose your team so that all the skills are represented. Encourage them to take advantage of their team membership to increase their skills in all three areas.

- *Mutually accepted working approach*. This covers things like how the team will make decisions, conduct meetings, communicate with each other and with outsiders (on project business), and resolve conflict. Some teams incorporate these into their charter as *Working Norms* or *Rules of Conduct*. Whether or not you formalize them that way, be sure to hash them out early in the process and get everyone's agreement. If you see people begin to stray from them regularly, it's time to revisit them and decide if they need to be updated.

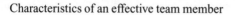

Characteristics of an effective team member

- Professes a commitment to goals

- Shows a genuine interest in other team members

- Confronts conflict

- Listens empathically

- Practices inclusive decision making

- Values individual differences

- Contributes ideas freely

- Provides feedback on team performance

- Celebrates accomplishments

Harvey Robbins and Michael Finley, *The New Why Teams Don't Work*[5]

I want it. How do I get it?

If you intend to build the kind of team you've just been reading about, there are a few more things you need to do to make it happen. These are adapted from a list developed by William Becker, president of Strategic Business Resources in New York:

- Allow members to express their opinions and ideas without fear. Obviously this precludes:
  - telling someone her opinion is dumb;
  - cutting off a member who doesn't agree with you;
  - interrupting or talking over people; or
  - laying blame if you try someone's new idea and it doesn't work.

But those are just the obvious put-downs. Equally devastating are some signals so subtle we're hardly aware of sending them: a smirk, a sideways glance, eyeballs rolling up to heaven, hurrying on past an uninvited idea. Any team member treated to these reactions a few times soon learns to keep quiet. Other team members who see these happening confine their contributions to those that match the sanctioned point of view. Commitment and accountability don't come to life in these circumstances.

It's not enough to avoid these behaviors yourself. You've got to see to it that team members don't treat each other this way. If you see that happening, tell them firmly that you really want to hear the speaker. Make it clear that you expect everyone on the team to show respect for the opinions and ideas of other team members.

If the culprits don't get the idea fast, take them aside later and give them feedback on how their behavior is affecting you and the team. Keep it focused on the behavior you observed and its impact, not on the character of the person you are giving it to. Here's a good model to follow:

"When you interrupted Roger twice, it was hard for me to follow what he was saying. Finally he simply gave up trying to make his point. It's important that we get the input from every member of the team, so please be careful not to do that in future meetings."

- *Encourage and reward innovation and change.* Banish the words "But we've never done that before," from your team's vocabulary. Unless, of course, someone says excitedly, "We've never done that before. Let's try it." Your team's whole reason for existing is to change something. If you let yourselves get locked in to the old ways of doing things, you'll get nowhere.

Where would the Trojan Reactor Vessel and Internals Removal (RVAIR) Project team have gotten if it had hamstrung itself that way? Winner of the PMI 2000 International Project of the Year competition, its purpose, as described by Jay Holtzman in *PM Network* magazine, was "to remove, transport, and dispose of a full-sized commercial nuclear reactor, complete with its internal structures and laden with radioactivity from 19 years in service, in one piece that when packaged for shipment would weigh more than two million pounds – 1,000 tons!"[6]

The advantages to this plan would be significant: reduce exposure to potential radiation for workers and the public, halve the radioactive waste, and save $15 million.

But – and a big "but" it was – such a feat had never been done before. Many said it was impossible.

Furthermore, the magazine went on to point out, "Several major pieces of equipment that would be needed simply didn't exist. And there were few regulations in place to guide the process. At the outset, it was anybody's guess whether regulators from two states and a confusing welter of federal agencies and departments would agree to allow the plan to proceed."[7]

Undeterred, the Portland (Oregon) General Electric team assigned to the task not only succeeded, they brought it in $4.2 million under budget, saving not $15 million over conventional methods, but $19 million!

Smart quotes

You can't solve a problem with the same thinking that created it.

Albert Einstein

• *Spread leadership across the team.* Don't worry. You can share leadership generously without losing your own. Leadership is not a zero-sum game. The more leaders your team develops, the more your reputation and influence will grow both within the team and throughout the organization. Give your team members every opportunity to develop their leadership skills by:

- Assigning them to head up subgroups. Try to give everyone such an opportunity.
- Rotating the task of facilitating project meetings. It develops them and gives you a break.
- Asking them to represent you in meetings with management and outside stakeholders. Of course you'll have to take them with you once or twice to give them credibility and confidence.

Your project team will operate most effectively if *de facto* leadership shifts, residing with the person best qualified to manage the task at hand at any given point in time. That doesn't mean you abdicate your oversight role. It just means you relax your hands-on approach.

- *Air disagreements and conflict in the open, focusing on creative solutions.* What is this? A couple of bullets ago we were urging you to make sure every team member could voice an opinion or idea without fear of belittlement or blame, and now we are saying, "Go ahead, let them duke it out." Isn't there some inherent contradiction here?

Not at all. I can listen to you respectfully without agreeing with you or pretending to agree for the sake of unity. If the whole team thinks in lockstep, that's not healthy cohesion, that's groupthink, an affliction that suppresses creativity, at best. At worst, it can lead you blindly down a path to ruin.

Expect intelligent, assertive people – the kind you want on your team – to disagree occasionally, and even to do so quite heatedly. The heat's OK, as long as it's expressed in terms of "how my idea will work better than yours," and not "why your idea sucks and you're an idiot for thinking it."

Respectful disagreement, even heated conflict, can lead to new solutions that neither combatant would have thought of alone. Made aware of a hole in her argument, a team member may find a way to plug it, or another team member may solve it for her. Both parties to a dispute may combine their favorite ideas into an even better approach, or they may both toss their ideas out completely and start over along a new track.

You can encourage a productive outcome by keeping team members focused on solving the problem rather than winning the war. In my book, *Recharge Your Team,* I reported this advice from a team leader:

"We teach team members from the beginning that it's all right to be emotional because you really care about what needs to be done," Haurin explains. *"But if being emotional about what needs to be done crosses over into being disrespectful toward another person, that's not all right.*

"We tell them to focus on the issue, not on each other," he stresses. "Because they need each other's help," he adds, "they usually are careful to retain respect for each other."[8]

Yes, sometimes conflicts get out of hand and threaten to torpedo a team, not enrich it. When that happens, there are conflict-management techniques you can use to avert pending disaster and even turn it into an opportunity for team problem solving.

Before punches fly

Actually the most insidious kind of conflict isn't that one that suddenly erupts into a screaming match with insults flying and arms waving. When the blowup is over, the antagonists usually respond to reason. It's tougher to handle the friction that never quite comes to a head, the one that smolders on with both sides doing their best to quietly discredit the other and line up allies. Meanwhile when they are face to face, the principals merely smile icily at each other. Confront them on it and they'll deny their own complicity self-righteously while detailing their opponent's misdeeds chapter and verse.

Whether you are dealing with fire or ice, before you step into the fray (except to keep people from literally punching each other), ask yourself these questions and choose the answer that is closest to yours.

1   Is it an isolated incident or a recurring problem?
(a) *It's very unusual.* Then, assuming there are no bloody noses, call a break in whatever activity prompted the fracas and give the combatants a chance to calm down. Chances are they'll come back anxious to move on.
(b) *It's getting to be a habit.* In that case, go on to the next question.

2   *Is team performance being affected?*
(a) *Well, no, not really.* Sometimes what looks like intolerable behavior to you is laughed off by other team members: "Oh don't pay any attention to them. They always act that way. They don't mean anything by it." And the people at the center of the ruckus blow it off and go back to work. If that's what's happening, don't let them dominate a meeting with their churlish behavior, but otherwise, ignore it. Well, make that a qualified "ignore." Keep aware and alert to any escalation or any sign that the strain is getting too great and beginning to affect the performance of the antagonists or anyone else on the team.
(b) *Yes. Progress has slowed down, people are avoiding working together, and team morale is sinking.* It's time to do something. But what? Try the next question.

3   *What's causing the problem?*
   (a) *It's hard to say. They just seem to rub each other the wrong way.* So it's a personality conflict or, put another way, a clash of styles. As Otto Kroeger and Janet M. Thuesen say in their book, *Type Talk at Work:*

   > *One person's laid-back style is another person's lack of motivation. Your thinking out loud is our annoying distraction. Someone's need to keep up with change is someone else's conviction to not fix what ain't broken. Those differences in style can lead to a great deal of misunderstanding, miscommunication, and resentment.*[10]

Smart quotes

Contrary to popular belief, the work of teams is not about togetherness, compromise, and consensus building. It is about hard work, conflict, integration, and collective results.

Jon R. Katzenbach, ed., *The Work of Teams*[9]

A lot of teams get to the heart of style differences with assessment instruments such as the Myers Briggs Type Indicator (MBTI). The MBTI is the granddaddy of such instruments and generally receives the most deference. It differentiates among 16 different personality types based the respondent's preferences on four dimensions: extraversion or introversion, sensing or intuition, thinking or feeling, and judging or perceiving. You can learn more about it and similar instruments online at www.aptcentral.org/aptmbtiw.htm. That's the Web site of the Association of Psychological Type.

If the idea of 16 different personality types each with four components overwhelms you, check out the instruments based on just four styles. One such instrument is the Personal Profile System, published by Inscape Publishing, which will reveal whether your behavioral preference is dominance, influence, steadiness, or conscientiousness.

Smart quotes	Most organizational conflicts are the result of personality differences that could have been resolved through a better understanding of ourselves and our colleagues. Power comes from recognizing the constellation of behavior patterns that swirl around work problems. Robert Benfari, PhD, *Understanding Your Management Style* [11]

Style assessment instruments are eye-opening and fun. They both validate one's own style ("Ya, that's me. Look what a great style I am.") and promote tolerance of other people's ("Oh, that's a real style, and all the time I thought she was just being difficult."). They take a little practice to administer and facilitate well, so talk to your training or organization development department if you have one or find a consultant who can help you.

Style analysis won't take care of every personality conflict, but you'll be amazed at how often you'll hear people say laughingly "That's a P [for perceiving really, but also procrastinating] for you," instead of getting angry at someone. Or catching themselves in a behavior or attitude others find obnoxious, and backing off with "OK, I'm being a D [for dominance] again."

Of course, every conflict isn't a style clash. Some are more substantive. What if your answer to the question, *What's causing the problem?*, is:

(b) *They disagree violently on what our next step should be.* Or, *we've only got one [you name the piece of equipment] and they both need it now to meet their deadlines.* Now you've got an issue that calls for conflict resolution. It's the team leader's responsibility to convert the crisis into an opportunity for team problem-solving so that the outcome is better than either antagonist would achieve by winning the battle.

Moving from catastrophe to solution

Your job is to help the warring team members:

1 *Define the issue in terms of a shared need*, rather than opposing points of view. For example, here's a shared need: "We're going to have trouble meeting our deadlines because, to complete both our tasks, we need more time on the [equipment identified above] than exists before our pending due dates." An opposing point of view is: "I need time on that equipment and John won't share it."

See the difference. Now the issue becomes, "What's the impact on our project if these deadlines slip and what can we do to mollify it?" rather than "I need that equipment more than you do." Now it's a team problem, not a duel between individuals.

2 *Identify the cause.* Beware: You'll have to remind everyone that the goal here is not to place blame ("John's the cause. He's hogging the equipment."), but to avoid bandaging a symptom only to be sidelined by a recurrence of the root problem later. Keep digging until you have the full picture. In our scenario, let's assume the equipment broke down and was replaced, sharply curtailing the amount of time available to John before the other person needed it. So the cause was a one-time occurrence unforeseen by the team, which had made no contingency plan.

3 *Apply consensus problem-solving techniques, covered in Chapter 7:*
   • *Determine the criteria for a solution.* Let's say our team agreed that the solution could not cost more than a specific amount. Members decided that meeting the final product deadline was very desirable, but perhaps not life or death. They considered the product requirements in the plan and designated some as must-haves, others as nice-to-haves.

- *Brainstorm solutions.* You know it works: no criticism, no judging. Hold everyone to these rules. Don't demand that suggestions fit the criteria yet. One person's suggestion to buy more equipment just might remind someone else of where you can buy rebuilt ones cheap.
- *Weigh potential solutions against the criteria.* Use the matrix described in the previous chapter or list the pluses and minuses of each alternative. Do the negatives outweigh the positives? You can drop those from consideration. Maybe one alternative will be the obvious choice, but more likely you'll still have work to do to choose among a few.
- *Agree on a solution.* Use the consensus-building tools in Chapter 7 to get the team to focus on points of agreement.

4 *During all the problem-solving steps above, keep two things uppermost:*
- *Focus on the task, not on personalities.* Each time you hear assertions like, "John always hogs the resources," remind team members their job today is to solve a problem they all share.
- *Listen to each other!* It's amazing how many arguments disappear if people just listen to what each other is really saying. One good technique is to get them to paraphrase their opponents' statements before they offer their own comments. If you want to take this method one step further, insist they not only paraphrase their opponents' ideas, but also find something to agree with. They'll have to listen differently to do that.

By the way, conflict resolution shouldn't all have to fall on your shoulders. The more a team coalesces, the more the members will view it as a team responsibility. In fact, you can pave the way by recommending that they include "how we'll deal with conflict" among their working norms. At the very least, that will give you a place to start your intervention when the screaming or the sneering starts. You can intercede with, "Look guys, here's how you said you wanted to handle situations like this …"

Key Behavior Agreements Required for Conflict Resolution

- Willingness to listen and to focus on the problem, rather than person

- Willingness to define the problem

- Willingness to allow some anger and hostility to surface during discussion

- Willingness to commit to decisions

- Willingness to accept that one might be a part of the problem

- Willingness to try to change behavior.

Deborah Harrington-Mackin, *The Team Building Tool Kit*[12]

Smart quotes

And finally, the bottom line

Is it a team yet? Oh, if you've come this far, you've got a team: dedicated to a common purpose, performing interdependently to meet goals, and working through conflicts to an increased appreciation of each other as contributors and as people. This kind of achievement deserves a reward.

There are rewards that are within your power to provide. Those are covered in previous chapters and include incentives that range from letters of recognition to acknowledgements in company media to celebration parties. There are also rewards you won't control, such as money and promotions. We could argue for a week or a year about whether these have any significant motivational force anyway, but whatever the answer to that, there remains an issue of equity. Teams and team members work hard, work in new ways, and provide innovative responses to company needs. They deserve to be rewarded through the same system that rewards individuals.

In organizations where management by project has a strong foothold, there are formal systems for ensuring this happens. In one technology company, teams are recognized through the formal semiannual reward process. The system is based on a point system: each employee can get a maximum of 100 points, and these are the basis for financial rewards at salary review time. The total of 100 potential points are distributed between team points and individual points. While team points include points for division and work unit accomplishments, a predetermined number is also allocated to project teams. To earn them, teams have to set bite-sized goals with well-defined metrics attached to them. Varying numbers of points are awarded for meeting targets, exceeding them, and for minimum success (hitting 95–99% of target) for each goal.

(Incidentally, while the system puts a cap on the number of allowable points for project teams, many employees volunteer to participate in teams way beyond the limit they'll be rewarded for financially. Perhaps that confirms that money isn't the best motivator. But don't assume it doesn't matter. *Not* getting money can be a strong demotivator.)

While every team member earns the same number of points for that team, teamwork affects the individual points too. These include a component that covers the individual's contribution to each team.

Assessing team processes

Making team success and team members' contributions a part of the formal reward program requires a fair and effective way to assess them. While the company in the example above focuses on measurable outcomes, some organizations also assess processes. It's harder to do, but not impossible.

You may ask, why bother? Ultimately, isn't it results that count? Well, yes and no. Results are what show up on the bottom line. But processes are what achieve the results and determine the team's credibility during and after implementation. Processes that cut corners lead to unsustainable results. Processes that hint at lack of ethics undermine the team's ability to get cooperation from the rest of the organization. Inefficient processes or processes that devalue team members contribute to stagnation or untimely demise.

You may want to assess your processes for:

• working together in a way that involves and shows respect for all members;

• gathering input from all stakeholders; and

• sharing information.

Clearly, it's hard to put metrics on these. "The team showed respect for all members 92 percent of the time," is a pretty silly statement. What you can do is determine the observable behaviors that contribute to the process and measure how consistently the behaviors occur. Here are some examples.

Behaviors that involve and show respect for all members include:

• Members attend all meetings.

• All members participate in barnstorming sessions.

• Members do not interrupt each other.

• They request help from each other.

- They volunteer to help each other.

Some behaviors for gathering input are:

- Team identifies everyone affected by the outcome.

- Teams interviews and/or surveys all those affected.

- Team obtains feedback from all stakeholders as work progresses.

Behaviors for sharing information include:

- Members report regularly on progress toward milestones at team meetings.

- Members with information request a place on the meeting agenda in advance.

- Members use all vehicles for sharing information: e.g. face-to-face, e-mail, dedicated newsgroup, intranet Web site.

Once the team decides what behaviors to measure, it still has to determine by whom and how. Most teams invite input from all team members, team leader, sponsor, appropriate stakeholders, and customer. There are a variety of methods to get these assessments, from team discussions at the end of each meeting (What did we do best? What did we do worst? How can we improve?) to forms and surveys to capture assessor input. Rating forms may ask the rater to assess the team on a five-point scale. It's usually best to have the scale rate how often the behaviors occur, rather than how well, which is subjective. The scale can range from "never" to "at every opportunity."

These methods work as a yardsticks for measuring team performance as a whole and for assessing individual contributions. However strong the team spirit may be, experience has shown organizations that people still want their individual contributions recognized. In fact, that recognition boosts their willingness to give their all to this team and to participate in another one.

One company's assessment system

In many project teams at GlaxoSmithKline, one responsibility of the implementation leader (that's what GlaxoSmithKline calls leaders of project teams) is to distribute and collect 360-degree feedback forms that team members use to assess each other's performance. The implementation leader forwards these to each member's work unit manager to be incorporated into the member's annual review. According to Mike Holveck in GlaxoSmithKline's Office of Change Management, the weight of these peer assessments on the individual's annual review is worked out with each manager in advance and communicated to the team member. Just what weight managers give to team assessments isn't consistent across the board, Holveck says, but "Typically, if you work on a project half time for a quarter, it will account for an eighth of your annual rating."

"Team members feel good about knowing from the start what impact their team contribution will have on their annual review," Holveck adds.

Real teams, while depending upon the willingness of individuals to put team goals above their personal ones, still acknowledge that it's the combined contributions of individuals that make the team successful.

The smartest things in this chapter

- A key difference between teams and other work groups is that members of a team need to interact with each other to achieve their goals.

- In effective teams, members hold themselves individually and collectively accountable for the team's success.

- Teams thrive on problem-focused conflict, but they wither under personal attacks.

- With effective conflict-management skills, project managers can help their teams use differences of opinion to generate creative solutions.

- Many companies have processes to incorporate project team performance into their performance appraisal systems for employees.

Notes

1 Katzenbach, J.R. and Smith, D.K. *The Wisdom of Teams*. Boston: Harvard Business School Press. Copyright © 1993 by McKinsey & Company.

2 Katzenbach, J.R. and Smith, D.K. *The Wisdom of Teams*. Boston: Harvard Business School Press. Copyright © 1993 by McKinsey & Company.

3 Bellman, G.M. *Getting Things Done When You Are Not in Charge*. New York: Simon & Schuster. Copyright © 1992 by Geoffrey M. Bellman.

4 Martin, P.K. and Tate, K. "More Power to the Team." PM Network, August 1998.

5 From *The New Why Teams Don't Work*, 2nd ed, copyright © 2000 by Harold Robbins and Michael Finley. Reprinted with permission of the publisher, Berrett-Koehler Publishers, Inc., San Francisco CA. All rights reserved.

6 Holtzman, J. "PMI 2000 International Project of the Year." PM Network, January 2001.

7 Holtzman, J. "PMI 2000 International Project of the Year." PM Network, January 2001.

8 Excerpted from *Recharge Your Team*, by Donna Deeprose. Copyright © 1998 American Management Association. Used with the permission of the publisher, American Management Association International, New York, NY. All rights reserved.

9 Katzenbach, J.R., ed. *The Work of Teams*. Boston: HBS Press, 1998.

10 Kroeger, O. and Thuesen, J.M. *Type Talk at Work*. New York: Delacorte. Copyright © 1992 by Janet M. Thuesen and Otto Kroeger.

11 Benfari, R. *Understanding Your Management Style*. Copyright © 1991 by Lexington Books, Lexington, MA.

12 Excerpted from *The Team Building Tool Kit*, by Deborah Harrington-Mackin. Copyright © 1994 by New Directions Management Services, Inc. Used with the permission of the publisher, AMACOM Books, a division of the American Management Association International, New York, NY. All rights reserved.

9
Representing, Relating, and Advocating

In the late 20th century, skunkworks came out of their basement corners and grabbed the attention of the business world. The idea was enchanting: free up a small group of creative people, give them a truckload of straw (and a moderate budget), release them from the confines of organizational bureaucracy, and – presto – alchemy would occur and they would emerge bearing gold.

We mention that only to illustrate what a project team is *not*. Unlike a legendary skunkworks, it is not an independent entity, operating outside organizational channels. Typically, it operates very much within the structure and norms of the organization of which it is a part. It continually relies on the support, cooperation, and good will of upper management and functional departments. It may also depend upon cooperation by external stakeholders: customers, vendors, even industry and community members.

Rules of Play

1 Help those who you would have help you.

2 Discover what they want that you want.

3 You are invested in their success.

4 Collaboration and negotiation are your best options.

5 Competition and avoidance do not work well for you.

6 Be open about how you deal with players.

7 Tend your relationships with key players.

Geoffrey M. Bellman, *Getting Things Done When You Are Not in Charge*[1]

Projects are very anchored in the real world. That's why many project managers find themselves spending a good deal of their time representing the project team to upper management, relating with outside stakeholders, and advocating for the team both inside and outside the organization. You may remember the comment of Rick Zehner, who headed Northwestern Mutual's Brand Equity Project, quoted in Chapter 2. Zehner said those kinds of interactions could have taken up 150 percent of his time, if he'd had that much time to give.

For something that time-consuming, you should have some guidelines. Let's build them out of the experiences of an actual team.

You can't do it alone – one example

How does a core team of just two pull off a $500,000 hi-profile project under budget and within a compressed timetable? By making the most of their relationships with people outside the team. At least that's the way Gartner's Alumni Connect project was brought to life by Kathleen Warren and Julie Viscardi, whom you read about first in Chapter 4.

Their experiences tell a lot about the importance of staying connected to all the stakeholders. There are lessons both in what they did and in what, in hindsight, Julie Viscardi wishes they'd done a little differently.

The upper-management connection

As project manager for Alumni Connect, a program to reconnect with former Gartner employees, Warren was in a somewhat unique situation. Her project was the brainchild of the company's CEO, Michael Fleisher. It was a situation with both advantages and disadvantages.

On the plus side, it made access to top management a lot easier than it often is for project managers toiling away on something obscure. Because he was passionate about the project, Fleisher spent considerable time with Warren when she took on the project, articulating his vision and explaining his objectives. With the tight project schedule and the CEO's personal interest, Warren didn't need the discipline of regularly scheduled monthly meetings to get his attention as work on the project progressed, nor could she assume such a schedule would be adequate. Instead, via face-to-face contact or e-mail, when necessary, she kept him regularly updated on the functionality on the site, deadlines, timelines, etc. "Michael's a very accessible person," explains Viscardi.

Even more accessible was one of his right-hand people, senior vice-president Zachary Morowitz, who could be counted on to have a pulse on what the CEO wanted and proved a great sounding board for ideas and concepts.

On the other hand, the CEO's avid interest also meant the pressure was intense, as was the scrutiny. If you recall, Warren was the project's second manager. The CEO had already had one unpleasant surprise when the first project manager left the company and he discovered how little had been done on the project.

Inter-team liaison

As you read in Chapter 4, Warren and Viscardi were building an alumni Web site at the same time as a much larger project was underway to complete redo the corporate Web site. The plan was always for gartner.com to "adopt" the alumni site, once the main site was up and running smoothly. It was up to Warren and Viscardi to ensure that their Web site was in sync with the larger one. "Both we and our vendors had to be sure that whatever we did short-term could be supported internally long-term," Viscardi explains. "If not, we wouldn't be able to offer it. We had to have two sign-offs all the time."

So Warren and Viscardi communicated frequently with the individuals supporting the gartner.com group. Sometimes it was hard to get their time, Viscardi recalls, but she and Warren persevered. "We'd say, 'This is what we're going to do. Can you support it?' A week later we'd get a yes or no."

Getting audience buy-in

The program they were developing was aimed at 4500 Gartner alumni dispersed around the world, so Warren and Viscardi made getting their audience's input and buy-in top priority. To reach these people, they started with the network of contacts Warren had built up in her 12-plus years with Gartner. Via her network and contacts of other highly tenured Gartner employees, they connected with a broad, international group of former Gartner people, many of whom had been with Gartner for many years and were still shareholders.

Warren and Viscardi reached out to their potential customers in some exceptional ways, including hosting dinners for groups in both the United States and the United Kingdom. They found out what people wanted and what they didn't want. Keep it primarily e-based, the alumni said, although they also liked the idea of sponsored events to draw people together. But they emphatically did not want to get lots of mail (postal) or fat alumni directories. They wanted to be able to search the alumni Web site for their former friends and colleagues, but they also wanted tight control over their own profiles in the database. People in the international regions in particular have very strong ideas on privacy, Viscardi discovered. They wanted to say whether or not they would be in the database and what information about themselves ("just their e-mail address or all about their five kids") would appear if they self-selected to be there. Warren and Viscardi built all of these functional preferences into the program.

The alumni they met with had other, highly practical requests too. They asked for discounts at Gartner conferences. Gartner Alumni Connect responded by offering free tickets to some conferences to alumni who met certain criteria. Everyone Warren and Viscardi talked to requested free access to research on gartner.com. That, too, they built into the program, again with eligibility requirements, even though they realized it could cost the company significant dollars.

Several months after the launch of the alumni Web site, with 1,000 registered users, Viscardi was satisfied that the efforts to involve alumni in the design and development of the program had paid off.

A language barrier

Communicating with their vendors wasn't always as easy. It wasn't lack of desire, nor lack of trying. But when bugs cropped up on the site as launch time neared, Warren and Viscardi ran up against a language barrier. Without technical background themselves, they just didn't have the words to express their problems or understand the vendors' responses. "We needed techie people to talk to our vendors," says Viscardi. "When I talked to them, it didn't make sense."

Spreading the word internally

Warren and Viscardi knew when they took on the project that their access to in-house technical resources was preempted by the much bigger gartner.com project. So they worked entirely with external vendors. What Viscardi realized later was that, by doing so, they were limiting insider knowledge of their project. While word spread broadly through the company about the upcoming new corporate Web site where clients would access Gartner research, comparatively few people had detailed information on the alumni project. That made her job more difficult when, as a last resort, she had to find in-house help to bridge the communications gap with the vendors and solve site problems that arose.

"Basically, because of other business units already committed to the launch of the new gartner.com, this project was managed through the Human Capital Management group," Viscardi explains. "Other business units were not brought in – until we absolutely needed them. Then we brought them up to speed very quickly."

One thing they did have going for them in that difficult period was the clout of the project's sponsor, the CEO. The weight of the CEO's name helped expedite many issues that could have stalled the project. But that was a tool they tried to use judiciously, to avoid causing resentment.

If she could do it again, she says, she'd spend more time educating internal associates, "so when we called upon any one group for help, they would have had a firm idea of the program, its objectives, and timelines to launch the Web site."

Part of advocating is making sure the team gets credit for work done. It's easy for the project manager to get all the credit because he or she has the visibility. As the project manager, you are in a position to make sure credit is given where it needs to be. In front of senior management, say "It was so and so or the whole team who had this idea."

Rick Zehner, Northwestern Mutual

SMART VOICES

Guidelines for managing relationships outside the team

From the foresight and hindsight of Warren and Viscardi, we can extrapolate these guidelines for managing relationships beyond the project team:

1 *Keep upper management and your customer up-to-date.* Don't hide problems. Your management may determine a reporting schedule for you to follow. But don't let your project suffer while you wait for a scheduled meeting to resolve an issue. Arrange for a liaison you can go to when you can't reach the highest-ranking person reviewing your project.

2 *Maintain links with other teams working with projects related to yours.* Even if your projects aren't as closely connected as Gartner's two Web sites, you may be able to cooperate with another team in some aspects to the benefit of both. At the very least you can avoid unwittingly finding yourself competing for resources, stepping on toes, or reinventing each other's wheels.

3 *Build relationships with your end users.* Treat them special. Use your relationship to get a confirmed handle on the users' wants and needs, to develop their trust in you, and to build up anticipation for your product or service.

4 *Find a common language with all your stakeholders.* The kind of miscommunications that occurred between the Gartner team and their technical vendors happen everywhere, over and over. We think we're in total agreement with someone only to discover, sometimes too late, we had completely different perceptions of our agreement. If you are working with people in a function you are unfamiliar with, don't assume your understanding and theirs is the same. Find an interpreter fluent in both functions to help you spell out your agreements in ways neither of you misinterpret.

5 *Tell the world that you exist.* Use every means you can to get your project out there in front of everyone in your organization. You may need their help someday, or at least their moral support, and it will be easier

> If Star Trek is right, someday we'll chatter away with alien species, understanding each other with no problem at all. But in the meantime we have to overcome the linguistic barriers between people who speak the same language.

Smart things to say about managing projects

to get if they already have a positive perception of you. Here are some suggestions adapted from techniques described by Jeff Ward, manager of High Performance Work Systems for Celestica in Toronto, Canada:

- Hold education sessions to describe what you are doing, why, and what organizational processes you are changing.
- Use internal newsletters or, if you have one, an internal video network.
- Get supervisors to describe your upcoming project at department meetings.
- Get it on the agenda for site-wide meetings. Have the top manager tell people what to expect of the project and what impact it will have on them.

Keep waving the flag

You are the chief spokesperson and public relations officer for your project. It's up to you to generate enthusiasm for your project to sustain it now and build anticipation for your end product or service.

The smartest things in this chapter

- Keep management and customers informed of both progress and problems.

- Maintain links with other teams working on projects related to yours.

- Build goodwill with your potential end users to get their input now and their patronage later.

- Wave a flag for your project throughout your organization.

Notes

1 Bellman, G.M. *Getting Things Done When You Are Not in Charge.* New York: Simon & Schuster, Copyright © 1992 by Geoffrey M. Bellman.

Part IV

The Skills for Staying the Course

The excitement of start-up is long over; the thrill of accomplishment is sporadic while the tedium of pushing ahead is constant; unplanned-for problems occur, and the end seems farther away, not closer. Then, that too passes and indeed the project does come to a close.

Chapter 10 is about beating the doldrums and leaping the hurdles.

Chapter 11 deals with grasping success, closing down, and finally moving on.

10
Overcoming
Obstacles

First, a progress check. Let's a take another look at the four project phases and re-orient ourselves.

	Key deliverables		
Conceptualization	Planning	Delivery	Closure
Project charter. Agreement on the purpose, intended outputs, and scope of the project. Constraints and assumptions you are operating under. Core project team. Commitment of all the stakeholders.	Project plan including project deliverables, tasks to be done, schedule, assignments, contingency plan, communication plan, and budget.	**Status reports. Project review meetings. Change requests. Updates to project plan, schedule, and budget. Milestones achieved.**	All deliverables to fulfill project goals. Final financial accounting. Full documentation of project. Final reports to customers and management. Celebration.

The project is still in the delivery phase, moving along pretty much satisfactorily. If your project is like most, by now you've probably had to adjust some deadlines and maybe renegotiate some budget items. Even the expected outcome may have changed somewhat since project inception. But overall, it looks like you've got things under control.

Smart things to say about managing projects

> If everything seems to be going well, you have obviously overlooked something.
>
> Another Murphy's Law

And then, just when you start to get complacent, more obstacles loom on the horizon. Some of them originate within the team; some of them hit you from the outside. Don't be surprised if one (or more) of these happens:

- creeping ennui and loss of focus;

- turnover among key people;

- people performance problems;

- product failure;

- changes in organizational priorities, leaving you in the cold;

- across-the-board budget cuts; and

- you're scooped and turned into an also-ran.

Let's look at what happens when these occur and what you can do to blast through the obstacle, climb over it, or slip around it and continue on.

Creeping ennui and loss of focus

Sometimes it is just hard for a team to maintain its energy over the long haul. Curiously, two very different kinds of teams are especially susceptible to doldrums after they've been active for some time. The first is a team geared to producing just one wonderful, difficult output. At first just being on such an élite project is a thrill, every small milestone is a cause for jubilation, and every problem solved is confirmation of genius. But eventually, after months or even years of intense effort, and with the goal still out of sight, a dulling tiredness can set in, stifling progress.

Smart quotes

In *The Soul of a New Machine,* a classic story of a determined team's struggle to produce a new computer, author Tracy Kidder tells of a time when enthusiasm waned and the team slowed down.

"It was an evening in August. They still had a long way to go. But, as if in concert with the season, the Hardy Boys were stuck in the deepest lull of their campaign ... 'Back in the early days, when nothing worked, it was easy to find things to do ... Now almost everything works ... The problems are harder to find ... They take days ... The people are more tired, I think ... The problems may be less interesting ... Some are more complicated ... This is the grind part, I think.'"

A little later, Kidder writes, " 'It's a long-term tiredness,' said Rasala ... 'It's a tiredness going home won't solve.' It fit his mood perfectly."[2]

The other kind of team that is subject to this kind of letdown is one that is charged with producing a lot of pieces, no one of them more important than the other. A team formed to produce a new set of marketing tools is an example. Exactly because it doesn't have one final transcendent output to look forward to, this kind of team can grind down after it's completed one or a few of its products. One former member of such a team in a publishing company remembers how a number of her teammates just slipped away after the team produced one product. As she put it, "It looked as if the team had just fizzled out."

In fact, it had. Shortly afterward it disbanded.

There are things you can do to keep your team from fizzling out. When you see that ennui setting in, try one of these:

1 *Change something to shake things up*. In *The Soul of a New Machine*, Rasala, the team leader, pitched in and joined the glazed-over debuggers in their daily grind. He wasn't as good at it as they were and he let them enjoy ribbing him – especially when he melted a chip's socket with a heat gun. Whether they appreciated his willingness to share their toil or they just had a good time at his expense, his change in the routine worked. Pretty soon the team was back full steam.

You can also try changing the tasks people are working on. Sometimes taking on something new is rejuvenating. But be careful. Do it with their agreement, not arbitrarily, or they may feel they are being punished.

Bringing in a new team member can change the whole chemistry of a team. At best, the team will be infected by the newcomer's enthusiasm. Or they may, probably unconsciously, perk up in order to show off a bit. On the downside, they may also resent the newcomer or simply decide to let the new kid do it all. You'll need to make it clear in words and deeds, both to the long-term members and the new one, that you brought the new person in to share the load, not because the team was incompetent.

2 *Refocus on a new goal.* For a team that loses its oomph after one or two small accomplishments, re-emphasize the overall purpose, redefine the team's goals, and establish an end result. In the example from the publishing company, this team did not seem to know what would constitute project completion. Its work had morphed into a thankless, unstructured, ongoing task – one with less priority than the members' regular work.

For a team whose final goal seems too far in the future to contemplate, establish sub-goals and make a big deal of them.

3 *Resurrect the good times.* Get the team together to reminisce about all the good things that happened early on. Determine the common ingredients and what the team was doing differently then. Sometimes it's enough just to remind a bogged-down team that, "Hey, we were good. Remember when we averted that catastrophe … ." That can lead to, "We can do that again. What if we … ?"

4 *Get advice.* Talk the situation over with your project sponsor, who may be just far enough removed from the fray to have a fresh viewpoint.

5 *Seek professional help.* This might be the time for some team-building activities. If your company has an organization development group, see what the people there have to offer.

Turnover among key people

SMART VOICES

Turnover is like a gunshot wound to a customer focus team. Every time you change personnel, team unity dies a little.

A team leader at Picker International

When a key team member departs, especially if the move is sudden and unexpected, the effect on the team can be unsettling at best, and devastating at worst. First, there's a knowledge gap. Even if you can find an equally skilled replacement, it's going to take a while for the person to learn the project and either adapt to his predecessor's way of working or convert the team and the project to his own.

In the meantime the fallout can come in different guises.

Scapegoating the dear departed

A team member who leaves can become an easy target on which to blame all the project woes. Unfortunately, this kind of indulgence burns energy the team needs to forge ahead.

Project teams at AXA Client Solutions often have co-leaders, one from the business side and one from the technology side. Vice-president Sherri Lindenberg was business leader on a team to launch an electronic document exchange. After months of work, the technology co-leader left the company, a disruption that threatened to throw the whole project into disarray. The change involved more than just one person, as the project moved to an entirely different IT group within the company. When the new people came on board, they could find no documentation of critical processes. It was almost like starting from ground zero, Lindenberg recalls.

At first, there was a tendency to point fingers at the people who had been on the project before. Lindenberg knew she had to nip that. "This is new territory," she emphasized. "We're learning from it." The team regrouped, rallying around a new short-term goal: to put in place a documentation procedure with checks and balances for protecting deadlines.

In 1999, as the calendar edged toward the 2000 mark, Megan Taylor of Gartner was leading a team called the Y2K Vigilantes to ensure the company's Y2K compliancy. When the project sponsor, the CIO, left the company, Taylor hit what she called the "Oh No Zone."

To the team, it felt like they were left holding the bag. On a project of this nature the support of senior management was essential, and suddenly their direct link upward was gone. But you don't have to be around Gartner people for long before you hear the words, "We're the Gartner Group. Of course we'll get it done." Taylor, supported by a new CIO who assumed the sponsorship role vigorously, rallied the team around that kind of company pride.

> Smart things to say about managing projects

Breakdown of team relationships

When one member of an interdependent group leaves, team unity is shaken. The remaining members reassess their own roles and their relationships with each other while they size up the role and position of the newcomer and their relationship to him. Sooner or later a healthy team integrates the newcomer, everyone shifting positions a little to accommodate him most effectively.

But before that happens, a cloud of old questions – once apparently settled – hovers in the air again and enshrouds every member:

- What's the new person's role here?

- How will she relate to me?

- How will others relate to her?

- How will that change my relationship with others?

- Will my role in the team change?

- How will we work together as a team now?

Meanwhile, the newcomer is asking herself:

- What's my role here?

- How will others relate to me?

- Who's in control over what?

- What do I have to do to belong?

Struggling with these issues, the team falls back to the first or second of the four stages of team development known as forming, storming, norming, and performing. In the forming stage, new team members are generally polite and cautious, feeling each other out carefully, assessing their own and others' roles in this team. After they've gotten to know each other better and feeling a little more confident, they take definite stands on issues and struggle for control, hence the name storming for the second stage. During the norming stage, they work out their major differences and move into a pattern of behavior – or norms – that facilitate their progress into the performing stage when the major work of the team gets done.

But progress through the stages of team development is never a straight line, and turnover causes some sharp zigs and zags. Members go back to polite, guarded interchange with the newcomer and occasional eruptions of frustration if the new member seems to be tipping the team's balance of control. Eventually, the team integrates the newcomer, establishes new working norms, and pushes forward again into the performing mode.

KILLER
QUESTIONS

> How can I rebuild the team after a member leaves and an unfamiliar replacement steps in?

There are ways to make that happen faster. Suggestions from successful project team leaders include:

- *Bring the new person up to speed fast.* Provide written documentation of the team's activities so far, then arrange for the newcomer to meet with a couple of team members for further elaboration. Otherwise what can happen is that the newcomer is left to find his own way on the project and the only way he can do that is by asking countless questions, much to the irritation of the other team members who are concentrating on their own tasks, often pushing against impending deadlines. Or, left to his own devices, the newcomer takes his assignments and does them his way, only to find they don't integrate with the work of the rest of the team.

- *Mentor the newcomer.* Pair the newcomer up with a more experienced team member for a while.

- *Guard against the "veterans vs. upstarts" syndrome.* If a team takes on several new members at once, there's a real danger of a veterans vs.

upstarts mentality setting in. Unless the team integrates them quickly, the newcomers will bond with each other, feeling less welcomed by the veterans. As a group, they may even try to press a new agenda since they weren't around to have input into the original plans and they've got some ideas of their own. The veterans, who have brought the team this far, may not welcome what they perceive of as interference by upstarts.

If the work allows it, pairing each newcomer with a veteran can defend against the emergence of such a "we-they" attitude. If you can't do that, make sure the new people understand the contributions of the veterans. And make sure the veterans concur on what's expected of the newcomers. This might be a good time to revisit the team purpose and redefine the role of each team member. That tends to dissolve the subgroups, advises one experienced team leader, and gets people thinking as individuals, contributing to the whole team effort.

- *Reassign the workload.* Unless you replace a departed team member with a clone, you are almost bound to have to make some task reassignments when team membership shifts. Unless the needed changes are very minor, bring the team together to review the goals, revise plans to take advantage of all members' capabilities, identify any skill gaps that may still exist, and determine how to fill those gaps.

Performance problems

Ideally, a project has a handpicked team of people chosen for their skills and suitability. There shouldn't be any performance problems among them. But in real life, such problems do happen. A team member falls behind on deadlines without explanation, avoids team meetings, and turns in shoddy or incomplete work. Another member, despite genuine efforts, fails to perform well enough to meet expectations.

> All projects are not blessed with superstars. In fact, many projects are not even blessed with average performers. Not only are poor performers nonproductive, but they also distract and drag down good performers around them.
>
> Joan Knutson and Ira Bitz, *Project Management: How to Plan and Manage Successful Projects* [3]

What to do? Before you take action, you need to uncover the reason for the person's failure. Is it lack of skill? Is the person under pressure to attend to other priorities? Is it resistance to the project or to the way the team works? Is it a temporary personal problem that's interfering with work? Your first step is to meet with the individual, objectively describe the performance problem, and invite the person to discuss the issue from her point of view.

When you've determined whether it's a can't-do problem or a won't-do one, it's time to take action. You've got choices about what to do, but it's a good idea not to make that decision alone. Get the team's input and your sponsor's before you take any severe disciplinary measure.

If it's a problem of skill, you could:

- *Provide training.* If you find out the person is incapable of doing the work, you may be able to help her get the skills she needs to perform up to expectations. Can another member coach her? Does the company provide appropriate training programs? Are there outside courses she can attend? Of course, you need to determine if any of these fit into your schedule.

- *Reassign tasks.* Although she can't do the tasks she's been working on, she may be able to perform well on some other project task. If there is someone else on the team who can take over the work she's been struggling with, you may be able to solve the problem by juggling assignments.

What do I do about a team member who just doesn't seem to care about the project anymore?

If it's a problem of will, you could:

- *Provide performance counseling.* Describe the performance problem and its impact on the project. Clarify the standards of performance the project requires. Invite her to make suggestions for what she can do to meet those standards.

- *Remove the person from the team.* If the person really doesn't want to participate and you can replace her, this may be the quickest and least disruptive solution. Bear in mind the issues that turnover can cause, but if this person has been holding the team back, it's likely the rest of the team will be relieved to see her go.

Product failure

Particularly if your project involves computers – and what project doesn't anymore? – there's a good chance that at some point, something you create is just not going to work. Not because someone screws up or does something stupid, but just because most creative work requires trying out a lot of ideas before one turns out to be just right. And it doesn't have to be a computer problem. Anything from a new lipstick to a new car is going to have its own version of "fatal error" at least a few times before the perfect product rolls off of the testing line. It doesn't even have to be a manufactured product. The best writers get their manuscripts back from the publisher with instructions to redo chunks.

When these setbacks occur, they're demotivating. And what's really dangerous is when you don't recognize those fatal errors soon enough and they get compounded in succeeding project tasks.

You can't prevent these disappointments from ever happening, but you can lessen their impact and reduce the chances that they will be compounded if you:

- *Resist placing blame.* Most of these interim failures happen because nobody's combined these particular components before in this particular process, so they can't guarantee the result. They are the result of creativity, curiosity, and eagerness, not malfeasance. Even if someone did make a mistake, blaming doesn't solve the problem. It just creates resentment and can generate crippling fear of failure among other members of the team.

Smart quotes

IDEO encourages its designers "to fail often to succeed sooner," and the company understands that more radical experiments frequently lead to more spectacular failures.

Stefan Thomke, "Enlightened Experimentation: The New Imperative for Innovation," *Harvard Business Review*[4]

- *Focus on solving the problem.* Turn successful rework into a new goal, and reward both the work and the ultimate success. Usually rework doesn't have the same motivating power built into it that creating something for the first time does. So pamper the people doing it. Bring them flowers and candy as they work. If it takes longer than expected, break it up with an unexpected champagne party – or pizza and beer if that's more to everyone's taste. Do whatever you need to do to maintain their willingness to keep trying.

- *Give the person whose work bombed first crack at redoing it.* If you turn it over to someone else immediately, that's like labeling the first person a failure. Everyone deserves a chance to convert a setback into a success.

- *Encourage people to report problems as soon as they discover them.* If people fear censure they will hide the next problem, hoping perhaps to solve it before anyone notices. But instead it will probably spread, increasing the damage. So reward the bug catchers; finding a problem is the first step toward eradicating it.

Smart quotes

Rework spreads like a cold virus. It isn't discovered right away and undiscovered, it spreads. In the Cooper & Mullen software study, rework on average for defense contractors took 9.5 months to discover.

Alan K. Graham, "Beyond PM101: Lessons for Managing Large Development Programs," *PM Journal*[5]

Changes in organizational priorities

There's a world outside your project, and it doesn't sit still and wait for you to finish. A project exists at the pleasure of a larger world, the organization of which it is a part. And sometimes the organization speeds up and rolls right over a project or makes an abrupt turn and leaves a project alone on the side of a road somewhere. Changing organizational priorities can inconvenience your project, transform it, orphan it, or even – let's face it – exterminate it.

Smart things to say about managing projects

You can't keep senior management from changing organizational priorities, but you can lessen the impact by staying alert to signs and preparing for changes before they happen.

This is a chapter about solving problems, but it's worthwhile to back up a bit here and talk about prevention. Granted, you probably can't prevent changes in organizational priorities, but you can protect yourself from being shocked into a reactive mode when they occur.

Some tips:

- *Resist the temptation to isolate your team* and ignore anyone and anything that doesn't directly affect the project.

- *Make it your job to understand company strategy* and take it seriously. Typically people below the top couple of levels in an organization think narrowly, assuming high-level strategy doesn't apply to them. But it does apply to you because you need to be able to explain how your project is in sync with it.

- *Stay alert to pending changes.* Gather your intelligence through every possible avenue: your sponsor, other senior management contacts, industry contacts, and the gossip networks. It's amazing how often people go around mumbling, "I never thought this would happen," when the rumors have been flying for months.

- *Keep aware of industry trends.* When the industry starts to change, your company won't stay behind for long no matter what people are saying internally.

- *Keep asking yourself, what … if?* If abc changes occur, is the project still relevant? If xyz changes occur, how can the project contribute to the new goals?

If you do all these things, then at least you shouldn't be broadsided when changes in organizational priorities occur. You'll be better prepared, but you'll still be affected by them to a lesser or greater extent. Here's what can happen and what you can do.

- *Senior management loses interest in you.* Project review meetings get postponed. Progress reports go unanswered. This may not seem so bad at first. If you've had senior management breathing down your neck, you may even feel relieved. But it's going to be hard to get help when you need it. If you find yourself competing with another project for resources, you're not going to win. If a work unit manager pulls a member off your team, you're not going to get that member back; you may not even get a replacement. At best, you'll toil away uninhibited, but your success will go largely unnoticed. At worst, you'll be slowly crowded off the map.

  What to do:
  - *Don't relish your anonymity for long.* Of course, all the first symptoms could just be a sign that management is so satisfied with your progress that it's focusing its attention elsewhere at this crucial time. But don't count on it. Get the real scoop from your sponsor.
  - *Plot your own strategy with the team sponsor.* With the sponsor, assess just how much support your project still has in the new environment and determine how you can tap it. Enlist the support of any leader who still loves you. Decide if you should you speed up, scale back, or make adjustments.
  - *With your sponsor, make your pitch to management.* Show the connections between your project and the management's new interests.
  - *Get all the publicity you can.* Keep your visibility high with articles in company newsletters, messages on the company intranet, posters – whatever media are available. Always make that connection to the new strategic direction.

- *Management changes your project,* perhaps beyond recognition. If you've been developing genetically engineered rhubarb, and management, having changed its religion, demands that you make sure it doesn't harm butterflies – well, that's one thing. It's going to slow you down, and you'll have to accommodate that, but to some of the team, anyway, it's going to be an interesting new challenge. But if the change is from genetically engineered rhubarb to organically grown horseradish, that's another story. You're expected to chuck weeks, months, or years or work, forget about the part of the project that excited you in the first place, and start over on something that just doesn't ring your bells.

What to do:
- *Keep an open mind.* Stifle your instinct to slam down your yellow pad and march out of the room. Give yourself time to review the idea objectively and look for the positives. What can you learn from pursuing this new goal? What can you salvage from the work you've already done? How well equipped is your team to take it on?
- *Negotiate.* Just because senior managers asked for it doesn't mean they are locked into organically grown horseradish. If you can find out what they hope to gain from it, you may be able to incorporate that benefit into your original project goals. Or, vice versa, you may be able to incorporate the benefits you wanted into the new goals.
- *Whatever the outcome, support it with vigor.* Don't make a half-hearted or cynical announcement to the project team that they have to do this dumb new thing because management says so. Approach it that way and you'll all burn out real fast. You don't have to pretend you think it's the greatest thing since penicillin. Just state the new goal objectively, explain how it reinforces management's new direction, and invite the team's input on how to pursue it.
- *Or look for a new job.* That's not glib, it's serious. If you really can't support the project change, sticking around will drag you and the project down. If your organization is big enough, you may even be able to find a new home for your original project within it. It's worth looking.

What if the worst happens and my project gets cancelled?

- *Management cancels your project.* Now don't close the book thinking, "What's the point if this is going to happen?" This is not an everyday scenario. Most management isn't that fickle or that anxious to throw away money. But companies merge, executives get swept out of office, and management teams do occasionally make major changes in the direction the company is going. So projects do sometimes get cancelled.

What to do (in order):
  - *Try to save it.* If you can see a link between the project and the company's stated new strategy, use all the suggestions listed above for saving a project that management has lost interest in.
  - *Propose a new project* using at least some of the members of your team. If you've been doing your homework you should know what kinds of projects would appeal to this new (or newly converted) administration and would use your own and your team members' talents.
  - *Close the project down, with pride.* Document the team's accomplishments, and make sure all the team members and management recognize that this project team did important work and learned a lot that can be applied in other situations.

Budget cuts

If you weren't born yesterday, at some point in your career you've probably experienced an across-the-board budget cut, when top management ordered every department, every function, and, yes, every project, to cut its budget by some fixed percent. Unless your project is very short-term or very, very high priority, it could happen to you. If it does, you can:

- *Make a plea for an exception.* It's worth trying. Crying probably won't help, but these things might:
  - Emphasize the importance of your project to the company's strategy and goals.
  - Demonstrate its positive impact on the bottom line.
  - Document how carefully you spend money.
  - Establish the detrimental impact the budget cut will have on your project outcome.

- *Search your budget and plan with a magnifying glass for ways to cut expenses.* Forget the paper clips; look for cherished nice-to-haves you can slash with regrets but with low impact on your results.

- *Determine how you can scale down the project* and still get a meaningful result. Revise your goals and plan accordingly and get a sign off by all stakeholders.

Someone else crosses the finish line first

It's the nightmare of every new product team. While you're still running tests and debugged your wonder product, Speedy Stuff Inc. scoops you and gets its version to market first. It can even happen internally. In giant companies, one group doesn't always know what another is doing, so two similar projects run concurrently and one finishes first. Sometimes management even pits two competing teams against each other.

It's a sad day, but wait, hold off on the laments. First isn't always best. Henry Ford didn't build the first car. And look at Microsoft. Can you think of a software product it brought to market first?

One benefit to being second is that somebody else has already created customer awareness. You can take advantage of that. When people know something exists, they immediately want it to be better, cheaper, faster, trendier, something-er. If your product is one of those "-ers," it's got a market your competitor made ready for you.

End in sight

After you've confronted and conquered hurdles like those in this chapter, you may feel like a battle-scarred veteran as you finally do approach the project end. So give a sigh of relief and a shout of victory, and get ready to finish up and wind down. The final chapter describes how to do that.

The smartest things in this chapter

- If listlessness infects your team, change something to shock members back into action. Then refocus them on the goals.

- Bring a new team member up to speed fast with documentation of what's happened so far and a team mentor to work alongside for a while.

- If a team member performs poorly, provide training or reassignment if it's a skill problem, and counseling if it's a "will" problem.

- If a product fails, don't place blame. Do give the responsible person the first opportunity to solve the problem.

- Stay alert to pending organizational and industry changes. Keep asking yourself how your project can support them or fit into the change.

- Don't despair if a competitor beats you to the finish line. Take advantage of a knowledgeable market awaiting an improved product.

Notes

1   Kidder, T. *The Soul of a New Machine*. Boston: Atlantic-Little Brown. Copyright © 1981 by John Tracy Kidder.

2   Kidder, T. *The Soul of a New Machine*. Boston: Little Brown and Company. Copyright © 1981 by John Tracy Kidder.

3   Excerpted from *Project Management: How to Plan and Manage Successful Projects*, by Joan Knutson, *et al.* Copyright © 1991 AMACOM. Used with the permission of the publisher, AMACOM Books, a division of the American Management Association International, New York, NY. All rights reserved.

4   Thomke, S. "Enlightened Experimentation: The New Imperative for Innovation," *Harvard Business Review*, February 2001.

5   Graham, A.K "Beyond PM101: Lessons for Managing Large Development Programs," *Project Management Journal*, December, 2000.

11

Crossing the Finish Line

Visualize again that giant network diagram filling your conference room wall. By now you've scribbled all over it, crossed out and redrawn parts of it, probably even torn down and replaced sections. But those meetings the team has had, with all of you clustered around the wall diagram, have gradually moved along it until now you are finally facing the box that says finish.

It's time for cheers and for tears, but wait, there are still things to do before you and the team strike out on your next adventures.

This chapter is about the Closure phase, when you bring the project to an end – although your output, hopefully, lives on. You and the team members may go back to being salarymen and salarywomen, as the Japanese say, or you may pack up your project management tool kits and move on to the next project. The table below shows the typical deliverables for this phase.

	Key deliverables		
Conceptualization	Planning	Delivery	Closure
Project charter. Agreement on the purpose, intended outputs, and scope of the project. Constraints and assumptions you are operating under. Core project team. Commitment of all the stakeholders.	Project plan including project deliverables, tasks to be done, schedule, assignments, contingency plan, communication plan, and budget.	Status reports. Project review meetings. Change requests. Updates to project plan, schedule, and budget. Milestones achieved.	**All deliverables to fulfill project goals. Final financial accounting. Full documentation of project. Final reports to customers and management. Celebration.**

Smart answers to tough questions

Is it done yet?

Remember the class reunion dinner from Chapter 4. If you were managing that project, when you woke up the morning after, you'd know it was over. Or would you? What about the bills left to pay, the thank-you notes to write?

If it's hard to close down something that straightforward, what about a project to create a new Web site? You get it up and running, but it can't just sit there, looking the same for the next year. So now what? Is maintaining and updating it part of the project? Does this project go on forever?

Q There's always more to do. How will I know when the project is over?
A Go back to your project charter and your project plan. They defined your final output. The project is over when you've completed that output. Anything beyond that is a new project or ongoing work. That's a new ballgame.

When the final output defined in your project charter and project plan is complete, it's time to close down the project. But that doesn't mean turning your back and walking away. Closing down can be almost as complicated as starting up. You may not need to do a new work breakdown structure, but at the very least, you should make a checklist of the items that follow and tick them off as you complete them.

What still needs to be done

You'll need to:

- *Verify that all promised deliverables are complete.* Go over all project deliverables with a fine-tooth comb to make sure nothing has fallen through the cracks. You may find a Whoops or two – What, there's still one more test to run on the prototype? Better get to it. Inevitably some tasks work their way to the underside of everybody's to-do list, things like final proofreading of a user manual that's been revised so many times it feels shopworn.

- *Create a list of loose ends that need to be tied off.* With the team, prioritize, schedule, assign, and do the actions needed.

- *Confirm with the customers, upper management, and other stakeholders that all project outputs have been accomplished* to their satisfaction.

- *Notify team members in writing when the project will end.* This shouldn't come as a surprise to them. The date is one they should have had input into. The written notification is for their records.

- *Notify their managers in writing* when the project will end and team members will be free to work full-time back at their work units.

- *Notify all vendors in writing* when their services will no longer be required. Again, this should be a formality, not a surprise.

- *Release any leased or borrowed equipment.*

- *Close the books on the project.* Complete the final financial accounting. If the project has a budget code, have it terminated.

- *Hand off responsibility* to permanent staff if your project turns into an ongoing program to be run by others.

- *Celebrate.* This isn't a fun option. It's as necessary as your final project report, because this is what really brings closure on the project for the people who worked on it. To close down a global project, Gartner brought people together from all over the world for dinner and for sharing experiences. After 18 months of highs and lows, frustrations and successes, now they remembered how much fun they'd had and talked about all they'd learned. They basked in the praise of top management. They tossed around ideas for working together on more projects. And as the evening wore down, they said their good-byes. It had been good, and they were ready to move on.

  You probably won't have to bring team members from Japan, and your celebration may be in the local pizza parlor. That's fine. Do bring in some top brass to give brief, heartfelt thanks to the group. Pass out some real and some joke awards. If you've taken pictures as the weeks or months moved along, do a slide show. Most important, get everyone talking, remembering, congratulating themselves. Ending on a high note prepares people to move on with energy.

- *Write thank-you letters.* Yes letters, on paper, in envelopes, with stamps. Support your local post office! Send one to everyone who touched the project – team members, their bosses, advisors, people whose advice you sought, managers who lent you equipment or office space, vendors, and, of course, customers. This isn't a form letter, though. Make each one personal, highlighting how that person's contribution helped the project.

Q How do I pass on what I learned?

A At the end of a major project you put together a historical document to show what you did, what your problems were, and what lessons were learned.

Charles R. White, PMP, RVAIR team planner/scheduler, quoted by Jay Holtzman in 'PMI 2000 International Project of the Year,' *PM Network*[1]

Smart answers to tough questions

- *Complete your documentation of the entire project* – the steps you took, the changes you made, the problems you encountered, the actions taken to solve them, the shortcuts and better methods the team discovered, the issues with vendors, what worked better than you expected, and what you'd do differently next time. All these things go into your historical record for the benefit of anyone who takes on a similar project in the future.

- *Prepare your final reports* for customers and management. At the very least these should include:
  - a summary of major accomplishments;
  - a comparison of achievements against original goals, final specifications against original requirements, actual schedule against the projected one;
  - final financial accounting with explanations of significant variances from the budget;
  - a description of how the project was organized;
  - acknowledgement of achievements of individual team members; and
  - recommendations for follow-up.

Especially for an internal audience, you could also include lessons learned, an assessment of the project strengths and weaknesses, and the techniques used to accomplish milestones and final goals. If the report runs into pages, prepare a one-page executive summary to go in front of it.

If your organization has an office of project management, that group may provide you with a form to fill out to formally close down your project and to contribute to a knowledge management system where project experiences are gathered and shared. If you have no such form from your company, you might want to use the following one – printed here with permission from GlaxoSmithKline – as a guideline to the kind of information you should record. At GlaxoSmithKline, this form goes to the Office of Change Management. Project managers may need to report separately to line management and customers, but after they've filled out this form, they're ready to do that.

Office of Change Management

Initiative Closeout

gsk GlaxoSmithKline

Initiative Name	Initiative Number

Close Out Comments

Describe if deliverables met requirements; Scope or requirement revisions; Budget or schedule variances; etc.

Cost Summary

Total Budgeted/Funded Amount	
Final Cost/Documented Savings	
Variance	

Comments/Variance Description

Additional Monitoring Required

Yes	No

Schedule Summary

Scheduled Completion Date	
Actual Completion Date	
Variance	

Comments/Variance Description

Additional Monitoring Required

Yes	No

Additional Tracking Required (Describe if checked 'Yes' above)

Lessons Learned

Team dynamics; Initiative timeline and controls; Requirements; Deliverables; Communications; etc.

Closed by:		
OCM Project Office		Date:
OCM Finance Office		Date:

It's over. Now what?

Smart quotes

Every exit is an entry somewhere else.

Tom Stoppard, *Rosencrantz
& Guildenstern Are Dead*

One project manager, blessed with incredible timing, finished up a company-wide, global project and went on maternity leave. When she returned to work several months later an important new project awaited her.

You may not be able to schedule your life quite that conveniently, but at least consider a vacation when you've nailed down a project that has consumed your time, energy, and thoughts for months or years. You're going to need some downtime or – if you hate downtime – a temporary change of pace before you reassimilate into ongoing operations or tackle a new project.

What you and your team members do when the project is over will depend upon how it ends. In project management terminology, projects end in one of three ways:

- *Termination by Extinction*. All activity stops.

  For a project like Gartner's Y2K effort, mentioned earlier in this book, this is the expected, successful outcome of activity that has no ongoing application after the goal has been met.

- *Termination by Integration*. The project team disbands and the organization absorbs the project activity, distributing it among existing functions.

  Here's an example: a project team made up of people from the training department and representatives from the line functions develops a management training program. Team members run the program for a few pilot groups, then train selected people from throughout the organization to present it to managers in their divisions. The project team relinquishes all ownership of the program, handing it off to the divisions to administer and deliver.

- *Termination by Inclusion.* The organization converts the project to a separate, ongoing program, often run by at least some of the project team.

That's what happened to Gartner Alumni Connect. It started as a project to get a Web site up and running and design a program of activities reuniting former Gartner employees. Now maintaining the Web site and planning and conducting events around the world has become not a project but a full-time job for former project team member Julie Viscardi.

In the Relationship Distribution Group that Greg Winsper heads up at AXA Client Solutions in New York, projects typically evolve into programs managed by the same people. "Our programs are a little bit outside the norm," Winsper explains. "There are legal nuances and marketing nuances. We tried transferring them over, but other people just didn't have the same ownership or passion. Meanwhile the people who developed a program don't want to turn it over; it's their baby. So we made the decision: Why fight it?"

So your project just might turn into a whole new job for you. But that's more the exception than the rule. In fact, many companies find that the best project managers don't make the best managers of ongoing programs. After a while they miss the challenge of creating something new.

The wiley.com/college Web site listed two other ways projects sometimes terminate. Hopefully, you'll avoid these:

Termination by murder

Terminating a project suddenly and without warning, usually for a cause not related to the project's purpose.

Termination by starvation

Cutting a project's budget sufficiently to stop progress without actually killing the project.

Your next move

Whether you ease back into ongoing operations or take on a new project (or a combination of both), life won't be quite the same after you've successfully managed a challenging project. You'll approach your work differently, and the changes will serve you well in any role. For example:

- *You'll think "scope"* whenever you are asked to do something new. Greg Winsper puts it this way: "Early on when an idea came in, I'd think, 'Yes, this is awesome.' Then before you knew it the thing would be huge. Now when a concept comes in, I immediately try to get the scope of it. That helps from a day-to-day standpoint. Now when people from the field come in and want something next Tuesday, I don't say no, but I do tell them how that would work and let them determine if they want to go down that path."

- *You'll do more planning and try to anticipate risks*, whether you are taking on a new project, or expanding your work unit programs.

- *You'll focus on results more.* Working on a project dissolves the typical operations mindset that views work as a day-after-day repetition of tasks.

- *You'll expect more from people* who work with you – more ideas, more commitment, more problem-solving – and, expecting these things, you'll provide more opportunities for people to demonstrate them.

Smart quotes

> As you gain skills in managing projects, your career prospects will improve as well. Management recognizes success and rewards it, and projects are an excellent forum for demonstrating your leadership abilities.
>
> Michael C. Thomsett, *The Little Black Book of Project Management*[2]

You make a mark when you successfully manage a project. You become known as a person who can get things done. If you don't get offered another project right away, and you'd like to take one on, look around for a problem just waiting to be solved or a customer need clamoring to be filled. Turn it into a project proposal. You've got contacts now to help you move it forward.

You might even decide to make project management a career. It is a profession now and not just in engineering companies. More and more organizations have offices of project management, staffed with people whose whole job is to work on projects throughout the company. The Project Management Institute is a good place to start looking for information. You might even want to become a certified PMP (project management professional).

With more and more companies converting to managing by projects, opportunities for project managers just keep growing. What you do with them is up to you.

The smartest things in this chapter

- Make a checklist of all the closing tasks and tick them off as you complete them.

- Make your documentation and final reports available to future project managers.

- Celebrate. It's important for moving on with energy.

- Give team members an opportunity to talk about what they've gained from working on the project.

- If your project turns into an ongoing program, expect to hand off responsibility to a permanent staff.

- In some cases, you and/or your team members may become the permanent staff for the program you created.

Notes

1   Holtzman, J. "PMI 2000 International Project of the Year," *PM Network*, January 2001.

2   Excerpted from *The Little Black Book of Project Management*. Copyright © 1990 by Michael C. Thomsett. Used with the permission of the publisher, AMACOM Books, a division of the American Management Association International, New York, NY. All rights reserved.

References

A Guide to the Project Management Body of Knowledge. Newtown Square, PA: Project Management Institute, 1996.

Baker, S. and Baker, K. *The Complete Idiot's Guide® to Project Management*, 2nd edn. Indianapolis, IN: Alpha Books, 2000.

Barr, L. and N. *The Leadership Equation*, Austin, TX: Eakin, 1989.

Bellman, G.M. *Getting Things Done When You Are Not in Charge.* New York: Simon & Schuster, 1992.

Benfari, R. *Understanding Your Management Style.* Lexington, MA: Lexington, 1991.

Bennatan, E.M. *On Time Within Budget*, 3rd edn. New York: Wiley, 2000.

Brown, W.J., McCormick, H.W. III and Thomas, S.W. *Antipatterns in Project Management*. New York: Wiley, 2000.

Caracciolo, A.M. *Smart Things to Know About Teams*. Oxford: Capstone, 2000.

Cusumano, M.A. and Selby, R.W. *Microsoft Secrets*. New York: Simon & Schuster, 1995.

Deeprose, D. *The Team Coach*. New York: AMACOM, 1995.

Deeprose, D. *Recharge Your Team*. New York: American Management Association, 1998.

Graham, A.K. "Beyond PM101: Lessons for Managing Large Development Programs," *Project Management Journal*, December 2000.

Harrington-Mackin, D. *The Team Building Tool Kit*. New York: AMACOM, 1994.

Holtzman, J. "PMI 2000 International Project of the Year." *PM Network*, January 2001.

Imperato, G. "He's Become Bank America's 'Mr. Project.'" *Fast Company*, June 1998.

Katzenbach, J.R., ed. *The Work of Teams*. Boston: HBS Press, 1998.

Katzenbach, J.R. and Smith, D.K. *The Wisdom of Teams*. Boston: HBS Press, 1993.

Kerzner, H. *In Search of Excellence in Project Management.* New York: VNR, 1998.

Kerzner, H. *Project Management: A Systems Approach to Planning, Scheduling, and Controlling,* 7th edn. New York: Wiley, 2000.

Kidder, T. *The Soul of a New Machine.* Boston: Little Brown and Company, 1981.

Knutson, J. and Blitz, I. *Project Management: How to Plan and Manage Successful Projects.* New York: AMACOM, 1991.

Kroeger, O. and Thuesen, J.M. *Type Talk at Work.* New York: Delacorte, 1992.

Lewis, J.P. *Mastering Project Management.* New York: McGraw Hill, 1998.

Martin, P.K. and Tate, K. "More Power to the Team." *PM Network,* August 1998.

Peters, T. "The WOW Project." *Fast Company,* May 1999.

Robbins, H. and Finley, M. *The New Why Teams Don't Work,* 2nd ed. San Francisco: Berrett-Koehler, 2000.

Rose, K.H. "Cover to Cover," *Project Management Journal,* June 2000.

Taylor, J.S. *A Survival Guide for Project Managers.* New York: AMACOM, 1998.

Taylor, J.S. *The Project Management Workshop*. New York, AMACOM, 2001.

Thomke, S. "Enlightened Experimentation: The New Imperative for Innovation." *Harvard Business Review*, February 2001.

Thomsett, M.C. *The Little Black Book of Project Management*. New York: AMACOM, 1990.

Weiss, J.W. and Wysocki, R.K. *5-Phase Project Management*. Cambridge, MA: Perseus, 1992.

Index